REST STOP AHEAD
SPIRITUAL REST FOR A HECTIC LIFE

JOHN SCALLY

HIDDEN HOLLOWS PUBLISHING

Rest Stop Ahead
© 2022, 2023 by
John Scally

All rights reserved.

All Scripture quotations, unless otherwise indicated, are taken from the Holy Bible, New International Version®, NIV®. Copyright ©1973, 1978, 1984, 2011 by Biblica, Inc.™ Used by permission of Zondervan. All rights reserved worldwide. www.zondervan.com. The "NIV" and "New International Version" are trademarks registered in the United States Patent and Trademark Office by Biblica, Inc.™

Scripture quotations marked *The Message* are taken from *The Message*, copyright ©1993, 2002, 2018 by Eugene H. Peterson. Used by permission of NavPress. All rights reserved. Represented by Tyndale House Publishers.

Hidden Hollows Publishing
Flint MI

CONTENTS

Introduction	v
1. Measuring Up	1
2. Overcoming Me	11
3. The Warning Signs	20
4. Boundary Backup	28
5. Calling an Audible	43
6. Stopping a Trend	50
7. Worn Out After Winning	68
8. Imitations Are Exposed	84
9. Fighting Disillusionment	101
10. Finding Quality Rest	117
11. The Ultimate Checklist	134
About the Author	147

INTRODUCTION

I still remember walking into one of my student's bedrooms at 7:00 a.m. on a Saturday. He was fast asleep, and I was armed with a leaf blower. Now, before you think I am some crazy creeper, don't worry - I was his youth pastor, and his parents were in on it too. I quickly turned that leaf blower on and watched him wake up in shock and confusion. That wasn't even the funniest one either. One of my other students had a plastic frog about an inch from his face when he woke up from the cold sensation of an ice cube against his neck. That Saturday was our youth worker's revenge day, as many different youth ministry leaders — with parental consent — "woke up" their students in hilarious and unconventional ways while video-taping the whole experience. In each situation, you could say that their students' sleep was dramatically and surprisingly interrupted.

There's nothing all that surprising about how busy we all are in today's culture. From travel soccer schedules to dance classes to band practices, our kids have us running everywhere. We live in a society where it has become commonplace for both parents to be working, and if you're a single parent, you're pulling "double duty." We have jam-packed schedules; we have important deadlines; we have extracurricular activities; we have demanding careers; we have crazy busyness. As a result of all of this, we have no rest. It's like being awakened prematurely. You know how that feels: you walk around the next day at work or school or wherever in a daze. You feel exhausted. You feel overwhelmed. You feel discouraged. You're on the verge of depression, if you're not already there.

There is hope for you and your family! The intention of this book is to bring you an action plan in how to overcome busyness. We're all "crazy busy!" I walk around my church, and I can see the stress on people's faces. So much to do, and so little time to do it. We all feel that way. We all seem to be living at 105% capacity when it's humanly impossible to go beyond 100%. So, what should we do? In this book, we will dive headfirst into the core issues of busyness and how to "contain" life. I've heard it said of great athletes, "We can't stop him, but we can hope to contain him!" You can't stop life. You can't completely stop the busyness of life, but you can learn to live within a framework that will bring you both achievement and spiritual rest. Today begins your journey from chaos to control, from discouragement to direction, from pressure to purpose. You can't afford to have your rest interrupted. **Rest is necessary for growth.** If you want to become a "better" parent, boss, student, athlete, musician, friend, or follower of Jesus, you must learn how to rest. It's time to take the necessary steps away from insanity into rest.

CHAPTER 1
MEASURING UP

When we think about being fatigued, we often think of the physical. We think of coming home from a long day at work. We think of spending countless hours studying for an exam. We think of helping a friend move his entire belongings from one house to another. We think physical. But could a major part of our restlessness be mental and emotional? Could our overwhelmed feelings have less to do with physical labor and more to do with emotional anguish?

In Jesus' day the religious leaders were really good at making people feel really bad about themselves. They were known for adding excessive and unnecessary demands upon the people. This resulted in frustration and discouragement, as these leaders were unwilling to help share or carry these burdens. It was exhausting as the people attempted to keep an impossible list of rules. For example, they took the Fourth Commandment to "keep the Sabbath Day holy" and added 39 regulations to it, even to the point of mandating "how many steps a person could take" (Midrash-Rabbi Commentary). I was thinking that guys could really take advantage of this rule by telling their wives that on Saturday they can only take a few steps into the kitchen for food and then back into the family room to watch college football. No shopping on Saturdays possible! Why? You can take only a few steps. Okay, I'm joking, ladies. But seriously, can you imagine using a day that was intended to bring man rest to make life more difficult? So, what would happen if a man's cow or donkey fell over a cliff? According to the hypocritical religious leaders, you couldn't take the steps necessary to rescue it. If you lost your animals, it was likely that you would lose your livelihood. This was just one of many examples of how these corrupt leaders manipulated and controlled the people. It led to unrest and discouragement.

Not much has changed in our culture today. People are always placing unfair expectations upon us. The question is, are we going to allow their unfair demands to control our lives? We intrinsically care about what other people think. Why is that? Because we live in relationships. Our relationships mean everything to us. We are fathers, mothers, sisters, brothers, bosses, co-workers, teammates, fellow students, neighbors, etc. We go to work together. We go to school together. We live in the neighborhood together. We go to church together. We are "together." There's nothing wrong with these natural realities until we allow "toxic" people to dictate how we should live. What is a toxic person? By my own definition, it is someone who breeds unhealthy values into your life. The kind of person who is prideful, arrogant, selfish, demanding, or comparative. It's the kind of person who could be a bad influence on us if we're not careful. Unfortunately, it's often the person whose affirmation we most desire. It's the person with whom we can become codependent for words of affirmation and acceptance. These religious leaders were those kinds of people. The average person wanted their acceptance. Their words carried weight. Unfortunately, they misused their words for their own popularity and prestige.

Maybe the greatest thief of rest in your life right now is people's expectations. You find yourself so consumed with what people think that you can hardly concentrate on your responsibilities. You wonder what they're going to think of you. You fear the worst. You hope that you can somehow "measure up." Just as Jesus' words were meant to encourage the people in His days on earth, they are meant to encourage you and me. Our focus needs to be on what He thinks of us, not on what others think of us. Jesus said in Matthew 11:28-30,

> "Come to me, all you who are weary and burdened, and I will give you rest. Take my yoke upon you and learn from me, for I am gentle and humble in heart, and you will find rest for your souls. For my yoke is easy and my burden is light."

The weariness had little to do with physical fatigue and more to do with mental and emotional anguish. Jesus offers his people recovery and an opportunity to collect their strength. The people were tired, burned out, worn out, etc., on superficial religion. Maybe you are too. Jesus offers a better way. The last part of those verses will be the climax to this book. Don't skip ahead. There's much to discover before we get there.

People's expectations take all shapes and sizes. It started for me when I was a teenager. I remember getting a "cool hair cut" back in the day. My sides were shaved, and the top was a bit longer. For the record, you must know that it wasn't a mullet. While some might have sported that pretty awesome look, that wasn't me. But I did have a trendy and popular look. As I entered the sanctuary of our church one Sunday, I had one of the deacons take me aside. He proceeded to berate me about my haircut, telling me that I looked like a "rapper" and shouldn't be allowed to have such a haircut in the church. He attached spirituality to a haircut. I'll never forget it. I walked away frustrated and irritated. Since then I've had many people in my life try to dictate how I should live according to their own man-made standards. The fact is people have opinions and convictions. Sometimes they forget which is which. Sometimes they confuse truth with preference. Sometimes they toss a burden on our shoulders that we are not meant to bear. It's up to you to recognize this and not allow it to control your joy. **God's Word, not others' opinions, is the only standard you are expected to live out.** Is it a jealous co-worker putting unfair pressure on you at work? Is it another mom you keep comparing yourself with? Is it an older parent who you are still trying to please as an adult yourself? Is it a peer group you're a part of that's making you feel insecure about your parenting skills? Is it your own kids? Oh boy, more on that in a bit. Buckle up for that one. Until then, who is it that's stealing your joy?

Jesus made sure that he exposed "rest stealers." Notice how he described the religious leaders in Matthew 23:1-4:

> "Then Jesus said to the crowds and to his disciples: 'The teachers of the law and the Pharisees sit in Moses' seat. So you must be careful to do everything they tell you. But do not do what they do, for they do not practice what they preach. They tie up heavy, cumbersome loads and

put them on other people's shoulders, but they themselves are not willing to lift a finger to move them.'"

Notice how they mixed truth with error. Jesus saw some of their teachings as good, but he also saw what they added to those teachings as dangerous. They were driven by their own agendas and their own power. They were insecure and motivated by greed. They set people up to fail.

Most of the people who place heavy expectations on us are the same way. We must recognize this. They're not motivated by compassion but by control. Their strategy is comparison. They always want you to look "less" than what they look. They always want you to look weak while they look strong. They always want you to look inferior while they look superior. Why then would you allow this person to "get into your head"? It's the kind of person who brags about their children's honor roll grades when she knows that your kids are struggling in school. It can be your adult parents criticizing your parenting skills when they also made mistakes raising you. It often is the co-worker or even subordinate who is so jealous over your success, he does whatever he can to make your job a living nightmare. Because we care so much about what people think, we allow their unfair and often inaccurate opinions of us to define us.

Live in healthy limitations by distinguishing between pressure and purpose. What I mean by that is be who God made you to be. You don't have to even attempt to measure up to people's standards of you. When you let another person's standard define you, the danger is that you'll always be chasing after an impossible goal, leading to frustration, discontentment, and ultimately to serious fatigue. How do you avoid this? Limitations. Limit your contact with toxic people. Limit your expectations of yourself with these people. Know the difference between man-made pressure and living out your purpose in Jesus Christ. The book's conclusion will focus on purpose, which is always healthy. In the meantime, man-made pressure can come from the most unexpected of sources.

Have you ever had an "aha" moment? You know — that moment of recognition or comprehension. That moment when you realized something you hadn't thought of. It can be exciting, like remembering a famous song from the past. It can be exhilarating like realizing that cute girl across the aisle is actually staring at you. It can be breathtaking when you come to salvation in Jesus Christ by faith alone because of grace alone. It can also be stunning and challenging. I believe this could be that moment for you. I believe this because I believe that many times the biggest culprit of placing unfair expectations on us comes from our own children. That's right, your kids. Face it, your kids demand a lot from you. It's not all their fault either. The fast-paced culture that we live in has somewhat created this mess.

At the swipe of a screen they have instant access to just about everything. More on that issue later. For now, the reality is that our kids have so many options facing them, and because of social media, it's always in their faces. It's like when I was a kid, and after church we would go out to eat at Sign of the Beefcarver. I would literally go up to the counter and start picking anything and everything to put on my tray. My eyes were bigger than my stomach. Our kids are no different all these years later. The only difference is that nowadays it's much more than food catching their eyes; it is travel soccer, dance classes, band practices, AAU basketball, karate classes, "underwater basket weaving," and so much more! You get the point. There is no shortage of extra-curricular events for our children. And, guess what — they want to be in all of them. They "deserve" to be in all of them. So, you extend yourself beyond your means to accommodate them. Why? Multiple reasons. Sometimes it's out of regret for what you "missed out on" in your younger days. Sometimes it's out of pressure that "everyone else is doing it!" Sometimes it's simply because you have not learned when to say no.

The price is fatigue. The reality is enablement. The result is disaster. You have multiple calendar events spending multiple dollars while creating multiple behavioral problems. You're not helping your children; you're hurting them. You're hurting the whole family. You're hurting yourself. Stop allowing them to dictate your parenting priorities. Just like when my dad told me I couldn't have that third piece of chocolate cake on my tray before I even ate the first piece, do the same for your kids. When my dad stopped me, I was mad. I didn't "like" him for the moment, but guess what, I learned that he was right. I couldn't handle three pieces. My eyes were bigger than my stomach. So, it's likely when you start telling your kids "no" that they're going to get angry with you. They might even start comparing you with their friends' parents. That's okay. They're wrong. You're setting important boundaries (more on that later) for both them and the entire family. It's important that you prioritize being a parent, not a "best friend" to your children. Our kids need leaders, not buddies. Our kids need us to tell them what they need to hear, not what they always want to hear. It's okay if they get mad at you. They'll thank you later.

Here are some warning signs to think about when considering whether or not your kids are "too involved" in extracurricular events: 1.) Do their activities interfere with family devotion time? If you're too busy on multiple nights a week to even read the Bible and pray with your kids, you have a priority issue. What do I really want my kids to remember about their childhood? That dad and mom went to their soccer games, or that dad and mom modeled and taught them the Bible? 2.) Do you find yourself resenting the fact that you have to "go to one more event"? Our kids' events are supposed to be joyous occasions. If you're not enjoying them, it could be because there are too many of them. 3.) Are your kids too busy to actively participate in their church? My dad taught me a valuable lesson years ago about priorities. I played baseball from the time I was a small kid until college. In those early years, my dad made sure that I played only a limited number of those games so that I could also participate in my church youth group. It changed my life. I learned that God came first and sports came second. I believe I'm in vocational ministry today partially because of that decision so many years ago. 4.) Am I living my own dream? We call that living vicariously through our children. Their home run is your home run! Their touchdown is your touchdown! Their first chair performance is your first chair performance! You get the idea. We live as if we're doing it, except that we aren't. It's awesome to cheer your children on, but understand that one day it will end. Have you equipped them for life beyond their extracurricular events? By the way, I have come to realize that almost all parents think their kids are better than what they truly are. This is dangerous thinking and can quickly spiral into priorities that ultimately lead to exhaustion.

You either have control of your kids' schedules, or they have control of you. Some of us are letting our kids do whatever they want out of guilt. This is wrong. Ultimately, you will pay a steep price if you're not already paying for it. It seems crazy, but our kids' expectations of us can be a real problem if we're not careful. Realize that part of loving your child is telling him no. If you choose to give him everything he wants, you will be emotionally, mentally, physically, and ultimately spiritually exhausted. It's important for us to remember what Jesus prioritized in Matthew 6:19-21,

> "Do not store up for yourselves treasures on earth, where moths and vermin destroy, and where thieves break in and steal. But store up for yourselves treasures in heaven, where moths and vermin do not destroy, and where thieves do not break in and steal. For where your treasure is, there your heart will be also."

My final warning about people's expectations is our biggest pitfall, which I already touched on: comparison. The fact is that we measure ourselves with ourselves. Comparison is exhausting. Here's a bit of advice that I'm still trying to consistently live out. You can always find someone more spiritual, stronger, more talented, wiser, and more attractive than you. On the other hand, you can always find someone less spiritual, weaker, less talented, less wise, and less attractive than you. It's all relative. The key is realizing that no two family stories, environments, upbringings, skillsets, bank accounts, or educations are equal. **Comparison is inaccurate and exhausting.** It's like comparing ice cream with pizza. Both are awesome, but they are different. Eliminate comparison from your life and your health will improve. I truly believe a correlation exists between good health and not comparing ourselves with others, because the worry and anxiety of always trying to "measure up" to someone else will be gone. Be who God made you to be! Be no one else. Did you know that the Apostle Paul also saw this as good and practical advice when he stated in 2 Corinthians 10:12,

> "We do not dare to classify or compare ourselves with some who commend themselves. When they measure themselves by themselves and compare themselves with themselves, they are not wise."

There were false teachers in Paul's day trying to criticize him for unfair and inaccurate reasons, but he didn't let that bother him. Instead, he ignored them. He knew that the only one we should ever compare ourselves with is Jesus Christ. When we do that, we fall short, which is perfect. Why? Because it's then that we'll strive to be more like Jesus, not another soccer mom, or co-worker, or church member, or next-door neighbor.

Do yourself a favor and exhale. You don't have to "measure up" to someone else's standards. As soon as you start believing that, you'll begin to experience much-needed emotional rest. The religious leaders of Jesus' day were putting all kinds of unfair expectations on the people. Jesus came to remove those unnecessary expectations. It's time for you to start living for an "audience of one." The good news is that if you know Jesus as your Savior, He's already accepted you. The challenge that we'll attempt to answer in the next chapter is have you accepted yourself?

CHAPTER 2
OVERCOMING ME

RIGHT NOW, you're thinking of it. You can't get it out of your head. You dwell on it. It holds your mind captive. It creates anxiety in your heart. It burdens you. You may even be dealing with depression over it. I'm talking about your past. Everyone has one. Unfortunately, for many, it still haunts them. It has crippled them in the present leaving them powerless for the future. At our church, we have an exercise that I have everyone participate in from time to time. I'll have each person during a church gathering tell the person to his left and then to his right, "You have issues." Everyone laughs and sometimes it creates an awkward moment. But then I finish the exercise by having each person in the auditorium loudly declare that he himself has issues. Why would I do that? To remind each one of us that we are all "broken" without Jesus Christ. When you come to that realization, it is then that you'll believe and accept His forgiveness for you. The Psalmist reminds us in Psalm 103:12, "As far as the east is from the west, so far has he removed our transgressions from us." Somehow, we can know the truth, but we don't apply the truth because we don't "feel" forgiven. This mentality leads to all sorts of fatigue and discouragement. What can we do to tilt the scale in the direction of joy? It's all in your perspective.

I was looking through some old photos the other day, reminiscing over my kids' childhood. From Halloween photos to Little League baseball to Disney vacations, it was quite the trip down memory lane. One picture, however, stood out to me. It was my son's first birthday party. No, it wasn't actually his party. It was the first time that he was invited to a party with his friends. He must have been about five years old, and the picture was of him and his childhood buddy Jonah. There's nothing like an invitation. You feel wanted when you're invited somewhere. You feel like you belong. There's nothing quite like it. Just a few weeks ago, a man in our church invited my son and me to go to a Detroit Red Wings hockey game with him. Wow! I was so thankful. I love hockey! It's actually my favorite sport, and the Wings are my favorite team. I gladly accepted the invitation and had a great time. It was kind of him, and I felt loved and accepted that he chose me to go with him to the game. It's time to change your perspective about you. Jesus wants you in spite of you. He's inviting you to salvation and purpose. He loves you!

Remember those hypocritical religious leaders? They were always making everything about them. Because of their selfish pride, they discouraged a lot of people. Before Jesus offered the rest in Matthew 11:28-30 mentioned in the previous chapter, He made sure to be clear who He was inviting to come to Him. Notice His encouraging words in Matthew 11:25-26:

> "At that time Jesus said, 'I praise you, Father, Lord of heaven and earth, because you have hidden these things

from the wise and learned, and revealed them to little children. Yes, Father, for this is what you were pleased to do.'"

Jesus offers an invitation today not to those who are arrogant and don't think they need life-change, but Jesus offers freedom to those who are humble enough to admit they have issues and willing to accept his forgiveness.

In God's system, humility is rewarded and honored. One of the best things that you can ever do is to simply admit your struggles, knowing that you have an all-powerful God to lead you out of those struggles into glorious freedom. What does that truly look like in our lives? Well, the answer is found in the Beatitudes. Notice what Jesus said in Matthew 5:3-4: "Blessed are the poor in spirit, for theirs is the kingdom of heaven. Blessed are those who mourn, for they will be comforted." The word for "blessed" literally means fortunate, "well off," or happy in the original language. What Jesus is saying is that true joy comes from realizing that you're "spiritually bankrupt" (poor in spirit). As a result, that realization produces a Godly sorrow (those who mourn) over your sin. Realize that Godly sorrow is meant to propel you to new spiritual heights, not to hinder your progress. No one wants to experience financial bankruptcy. But spiritual bankruptcy means everything, because you can't gain joy until you lose your own misplaced values. It seems like an oxymoron, but when you're "broken" over your sin, you actually are on the right road toward spiritual rest. How is that possible? Because you'll stop trying in your own power to reach an unreachable God. He can only be reached in your brokenness. That's liberating when you don't have to keep reaching in your own power.

You don't need to prove yourself; you need to give yourself to God. Have you ever felt like you had to prove yourself to someone? When I was a kid, I remember having a buddy over to my house. I really liked this kid, and I wanted him to like me. He was funny. He was crazy. He was cool. So, I felt as though I needed to prove myself to him. I remember that Friday night when, with a sly look on his face, he talked me into doing something stupid. He thought it would be hilarious if I locked my sister in the basement closet. I knew that was a bad idea, but because I wanted to prove myself to him, I did it. You can only imagine how well that turned out when she started screaming, and my parents came running downstairs. Ultimately, it was less about my friend and more about my mentality. I needed to see myself differently. I learned that night that human acceptance can be fleeting and superficial. One of the biggest problems that we often have is that we let others shape our view of ourselves. We're always chasing after their acceptance, as we talked about in the previous chapter. Chasing the acceptance of others leads us into always trying to "make God happy with us" as well. Think through this question: How can we believe that salvation is a gift from God by grace through faith, but then fail to apply that mentality to our Christian walk? In other words, if you didn't do anything in your own power to gain salvation, there is nothing you can do in your own power to keep it. Why is this important? Because God's grace not only saves us, but it also sustains us even in our weaknesses and mistakes. You are going to make mistakes. You can't dwell on your failures. Failure is one of the greatest teachers. What's next?

I'll never forget watching the 1989 Basketball National Championship game. It pitted my beloved Michigan

Wolverines versus the Seton Hall Pirates. The game came down to the end, when Point Guard Rumeal Robinson was fouled with three seconds to go in the game. He came to the foul line with a "one and one," with our team down by one point. I'll never forget that moment as I crouched down into a chair afraid to watch. If he missed that first free throw, the game was likely over, and my team would lose. Well, it turned out to be a special moment as he calmly swished both free throws. After Seton Hall's desperation heave from just over mid-court missed, my favorite team had won its first and only basketball National Championship. Can you imagine if he would have missed those free throws? Well, he did, just not on that night. A few months previous to that big game, Michigan had gone on the road to play at Wisconsin. Just like the Seton Hall game, it came down to Rumeal Robinson on the foul line in a one-point game. Just like the Seton Hall game, he had a "one and one." Unlike the Seton Hall game, he missed the first shot, and Wisconsin rebounded the ball and the game ended in defeat. Pandemonium broke out as the students rushed the floor; Rumeal had failed his team. It was a watershed moment in his career. He could have hung his head and quit. He could have allowed his failure to defeat him. Instead, he went into the gym before anyone else every single day and shot free throws. He shot hundreds of free throws. He resolved to get better. He resolved that if the situation presented itself again, the next time he would be ready. The next time he would succeed. It's amazing to think that it did happen again. Except this time the stakes were much higher. This time it was for a college national championship. This time he did indeed succeed.

This basketball story is but a microcosm of what is supposed to happen in life. You will fail. But, when you do, you're either going to become depressed or resolute. You're either going to become devastated or determined. You're either going to become exhausted or strengthened. If there was ever a man who started out as a failure, it was the Apostle Paul. Before he became one of the greatest Christians to ever live, he actually persecuted them. It wasn't until God actually knocked him to the ground on the road to Damascus that he realized what he was and what he had done. It's amazing to think that at some level Paul carried that reality with him his entire life. That's why he would later describe himself as the "worst of sinners" (1 Timothy 1:15) to his young protégé Timothy. But don't miss the fact that while Paul would never forget his past, he hardly allowed it to hinder his future.

We need to take the same mindset of the great apostle when he proclaimed in Philippians 3:13-14,

> "Brothers and sisters, I do not consider myself yet to have taken hold of it. But one thing I do: Forgetting what is behind and straining toward what is ahead, I press on toward the goal to win the prize for which God has called me heavenward in Christ Jesus."

He was able to set aside the past.

If you want to find true rest, you must be able to "move forward" in your life. What does that look like? Well, there are opposite extremes to avoid. First of all, the painful past. The fact is, a great number of people have a hard time getting over their mistakes. Maybe that's you. It's easy to dwell on a sinful past. I've had conversations over the years with people who didn't understand how God could ever forgive them. They thought their sin was too heinous. They clearly struggled to understand grace. Think back to the

Apostle Paul. He was an evil character before he was saved. He literally had Christians tortured, persecuted, and ultimately murdered. Do you think that reality ever truly left him? Maybe he never mentally forgot it, but he did spiritually move beyond it. Understand this: there is nothing too terrible from your past that could keep God from wholly forgiving you! Remember again what King David said in Psalm 103:11-12:

> "For as high as the heavens are above the earth, so great is his love for those who fear him; as far as the east is from the west, so far has he removed our transgressions from us."

In my counseling sessions, I've often asked people, after reading this verse, to tell me the distance from the east to the west. It's really funny to watch some of their expressions and responses. Sometimes I've even had people try to give me a measurement. The reality is that the east and the west cannot be measured. When you were saved in Jesus, your sin was eliminated from your life. You were and are forgiven. **Jesus offers true satisfaction to your soul.** Some of you are living in guilt over your past sins, but Jesus offers grace for your present purpose! You can lay that burden down. Jesus accepts you.

Secondly, move beyond the "glory days." You know what I'm talking about. It's the person who lives in his past successes. He measures everything by the past. All he can talk about is what he "used to do." It's as if he feels like he paid his dues and wants everyone to know. Understand that until you've breathed your last breath, you have a responsibility to serve Jesus in some way. My wife, Tami, often tells the story of an older pastor who had a profound impact on her life during her impressionable teenage years. He saw something in her and was instrumental in my wife's decision to surrender her life for vocational ministry. Good thing he didn't "punch the clock" and let everyone know he was done. Maybe I wouldn't be married to my incredible partner today if it wasn't for that Godly older man. You may have personally led hundreds or even thousands to Christ in your lifetime. That is amazing, but there are billions of people who still need Jesus. I love the fact that the Apostle Paul served Jesus until his last breath. In a Roman prison about to be executed, he proclaimed in 2 Timothy 4:7, "I have fought the good fight, I have finished the race, I have kept the faith." It seems like an oxymoron, but it's not time to rest! Okay, now I may have you confused. What I mean is that true rest comes in purposeful living. Some of the most discouraging times in my life have come when I was complacent and lazy. True rest is intrinsically connected to purpose. The past is meant to be our education, not our downfall. Success is meant to be built upon. What has happened in the past—good or bad—is over. Move on.

So what are some final thoughts on how to "overcome me"? Sometimes the greatest cause of unrest in our lives is chaos. Try simplifying things. We'll talk about this subject much more in a later chapter, but for now learn the basics of this principle. **Rest comes from clarity, not complication.** Learn to take it one day at a time. I know it's cliché, but it actually works. Focus on one task at a time.

Don't try to solve every problem in your life today. You can't fix the company overnight. You can't teach your kid to ride a bike the first time out. You can't renovate your house in a week. Change takes place over time. Remember, God is calling us to depend on Him. That challenge can be met only when we are willing to be transparent and vulnerable.

The wise words of Solomon in Proverbs 3:5-6 must be heeded: "Trust in the Lord with all your heart and lean not on your own understanding; in all your ways submit to him, and he will make your paths straight." Trust God, not others' faulty views of you. Trust God, not your own misleading heart. Trust God; He is available to you every single day. Jesus made this truth clear in Matthew 6:33-34:

> "But seek first his kingdom and his righteousness, and all these things will be given to you as well. Therefore do not worry about tomorrow, for tomorrow will worry about itself. Each day has enough trouble of its own."

What were the things that Jesus was promising to give? The answer is all of the things that we tend to worry about, like our health, paying our bills, food on the table, etc. Jesus makes it clear that if we could limit our focus on the challenges that each day presents, we'd be less stressed out and better able to trust Him. We'd see the "light at the end of the tunnel" for that day. We'd see each day as actually achievable. That clarity leads to a quiet confidence. That leads to encouraging peace. That leads to the calming rest that we're all seeking.

CHAPTER 3
THE WARNING SIGNS

SEVERAL YEARS ago now I remember being introduced to the story of the *Titanic*. I couldn't help but immerse myself in the details. What I found was a lot of negligence when it came to the inevitable reality of what was coming and then what happened. There were warning signs that were ignored.

As *Titanic* left Queenstown, Ireland, the radio traffic had consisted mainly of messages to and from passengers. It was the job of the operators to intercept messages for their ship and also to intercept general messages and warnings regarding the area the ship was sailing into, a kind of advanced warning. Each radio station had its own call letters, 'MGY' being the ones assigned to *Titanic*, and 'MKC' was her sister vessel *Olympic*. As well as the call letters, *Titanic* was also assigned 'ADVISELUM,' this being the code-word for passengers' private messages. Ice is a seasonal hazard in the unforgiving winter seas of the North Atlantic, and in the couple of days since leaving Southampton, many ships had reported ice in the exact area into which *Titanic* would be sailing. On the 11th of April, she received 6 warnings from ships stopped in, or passing through, heavy ice. There were 5 more on the 12th, 3 more on the 13th, and 7 on the 14th. All of these messages would have been written down as they were intercepted, logged in the radio book, and passed on to the officers on the bridge. There was now no way that the Captain, along with the officers, would have been unaware of the huge field of ice that now lay directly in front of *Titanic*. [1]

How could all of these warnings have been ignored? In order to answer this question, we must change how we view the process. Remember, the mindset from the very beginning was this:

When the British ship *Titanic* steamed out of Southampton bound for New York on April 10, 1912, it was the largest and most sumptuous luxury liner that had ever sailed. It was a monument to the promise of technology and to Victorian elegance, magnificently appointed with oriental carpets and crystal chandeliers. It was thought to be unsinkable. One of the employees declared, "Not even God himself could sink this ship." [2]

One of the biggest problems that we face in life is a combination of ignorance and arrogance. We believe that we're above the pressure. We believe that we can easily "suck it up" and keep charging forward. We believe that we're "indestructible" as the leaders of the *Titanic* believed. We get to the place where the warning sirens are blaring, but we're not listening to them. How many times do those close to us see our glaring issues to which we are completely oblivious? Right now, your family and friends could be concerned for you. Maybe they are sensing a loss of joy in your facial expressions. Maybe they are seeing an impatience that's led to a shortness with others that they've never before witnessed. Maybe they are noticing that you're not as sharp mentally as you used to be, forgetting the most basic of details. Maybe you simply don't see it. Maybe you do see it, but you feel "boxed in" with seemingly few alternatives.

It's so easy to simply start believing the lie that this is just "how it's supposed to be." In other words, "I have children; I'm not going to get rest." "I have a career; I'm not going to get relief." "I have responsibilities; it's supposed to be overwhelming." Most of us have learned to be "professional jugglers." All we ever seem to do is juggle. We juggle work, school, hobbies, church, meals, etc. That's just you! Now, put your family into the mix. Let me know if this sounds like you: *At work by 7 AM, Junior texts you at 8:30 AM telling you he forgot his lunch, head to staff meeting at 9 AM, head to Junior's school at 11:45 AM to bring him lunch, get off work 30 minutes early at 4 PM to bring Sissy to dance class, go to Junior's soccer game at 5 PM, eat dinner in the car between 4-5 PM, pick up Sissy from dance class at 6 PM (leaving at halftime), get back to Junior's game, get everyone in the car and head home by 7 PM, get showers, do homework, finish impossible science project, have a quick family Bible time, get kids in bed by 9 PM, you get in bed by 11 PM. The next day...REPEAT!* If you feel as if your life in some way resembles this example, raise your hand, or to feel better, just yell as loud as you can at the cat. Okay, that probably didn't exactly help. Do you know what would help? Clarity. Seeing the fog of frustration cleared up is our main goal. It's possible. Believe it.

Remember, the biggest failure of the crew of the *Titanic* was ignoring the warning signs. Maybe you're thinking right now that you don't even know where to begin. That makes a lot of sense actually.

We naturally struggle with the idea of "rest." Whether as a young child wanting to play or as an adult not knowing when to take a break, we find ourselves moody, frustrated, and ultimately exhausted because we live "unrested." **Rest is connected to the spiritual.** Remember what was said about Jesus in his childhood development in Luke 2:52: "And Jesus grew in wisdom [mental] and stature [physical], and in favor with God [spiritual] and man [social]." Notice the power of balance in that verse. You can't ignore rest. When there is a lack of proper rest, there will be serious breakdowns in other important areas of your life. How many times have we fallen asleep while driving only to miraculously wake up before we got into a serious accident? Did you know that a lack of rest is a leading cause of heart disease? Fatigue causes depression, ages your skin, causes weight gain, and much more.[3] Let's face it—sometimes our greatest enemy is ourselves. But have no fear, because this is where the Word of God becomes our guide into rest.

One of the hardest things for us to do is to slow down when things are going well. Jesus and His disciples knew this challenge. He had sent them out to heal the sick, cast out demons, and ultimately to bring people to repentance in Him. This was intensive work. This was demanding work. This was also rewarding work. It's really hard to slow down if you're experiencing success. Remember, as we stated before, it's easy to feel a sense of false urgency, where if you don't act in the moment, you could begin to believe that you're going to miss the opportunity. So, notice how Jesus handled this intensity in Mark 6:30-32:

> "The apostles gathered around Jesus and reported to him all they had done and taught. Then, because so many people were coming and going that they did not even have a chance to eat, he said to them, "Come with me by

yourselves to a quiet place and get some rest." So they went away by themselves in a boat to a solitary place."

Did you catch that? Great things were happening, but they didn't even have time to go through the drive-thru at McDonald's to get a burger. There was no time to eat. How many times have you cheated the basic necessities of life to "get ahead?" Sometimes we're succeeding in life in the present while we're cheating our futures. God never intended for us to do this. The reality is that it will catch up with us. It always does. It sometimes does in the worst kind of way.

One of the most difficult moments of my life came one rainy night on my way to the church. I was super excited to be meeting with some guys who were craving discipleship. They were interested in taking their faith to the next level, and I was ready to help them. As I entered the parking lot, my phone began to buzz. I looked down and noticed that my mother was calling me. I quickly considered ignoring her call, but then I began to think it might be an important call. What happened next will forever be embedded in my memory. I answered the phone, and my mom frantically begged me to pray for my sister. She had gone into cardiac arrest, and the paramedics were on their way. I was completely shocked. My sister had just a few months earlier been diagnosed with Leukemia. That day was a difficult day, but nothing like this night. I did my best to calm my mother down, and I began to pray for God to save my sister's life. I got off the phone with my mother, and I gingerly walked into the church building. I quickly met the men and began to explain what was happening. With looks of confusion and fear on their faces, they prayed for me and my family. Our meeting was cut short. Not too much time later, my father called to give me the devastating news. My sister was gone. She was with Jesus.

The shocking part of the story isn't even that my sister died. It's that she died one day after being cleared by her doctors of Leukemia. That's right! She was declared healthy just one day before she died. The reality is that she didn't die of Leukemia that night. Instead, she died of something that inconspicuously caught up to her—her lifestyle. My sister was single, and she lived like it. It was not uncommon for her to come home from her third shift after work only to head over to our school's basketball games. She ate Taco Bell like she had stock in it, and she rarely took time to take care of herself. If I had to guess, she averaged less than five hours of sleep per night. She rarely, if ever, rested. It's one thing to live that way during the summer of your sophomore year of high school; it's a totally different thing when you're pushing forty years old. For some of us, we are still living as if we are adolescents. Pulling all-nighters with buckets of Starbucks flowing down your throat while "living on adrenaline" is a young man's lifestyle that eventually needs to end. Matter of fact, don't even begin it. You and I need rest. My sister ignored the very basics of life. The heart attack that took her life was a direct result of underestimating the basic necessities of life. I wish I would have taken more time to warn her of the possibilities. She is greatly missed!

The toughest part of the story is that my sister was doing good things. Those basketball games that she was attending were to support and inspire a group of young girls that she had been mentoring. She was often sacrificing sleep so that she could volunteer in our home church's youth ministry. There were plenty of times when she sat with high school girls in fast food restaurants sharing the very wisdom that she ended up ignoring. **Too much good can transition into bad.** It doesn't matter what you are doing. You can't be all things to all people. You can't run, run, run without rest. You can't cheat the built-in boundaries that God has established and get away with it unscathed.

Jesus saw the warning signs. The disciples needed to eat; they had no time to eat. That's unacceptable. Evaluate your life. If you find yourself struggling to have time for the basic necessities of life like eating, sleeping, and even using the bathroom, then you're in trouble. I have literally been so busy at times that I didn't even want to stop to use the bathroom. That was ridiculous! Can you imagine being that unhealthy in your mindset? No longer do I live in such foolishness. Stop "cheating" rest!

The people who love you the most often see the warning signs in your life. When they decide to lovingly confront you, be humble enough to pay attention with an intention to apply their advice. Your health depends on it. With that said, there are also some warning signs that you are capable of seeing yourself. The next time you go on vacation, pay attention to whether you're actually resting. The easiest way to do that is to notice how often you're glued to that little device that fits so neatly in your pocket. If you can hardly put your cellphone down on vacation, you have a problem. In almost every situation, that email, phone call, or text message can wait. It's not fair to your family. They deserve more. It's not fair to you. You need more—rest, that is. Do yourself a favor and be proactive in this type of situation. Before you leave for vacation, warn your co-workers and clients that you'll be unavailable barring an emergency. Then make sure it is only an emergency that will get your attention. One of the saddest things is when a father on a family vacation is so preoccupied with work back home that he forfeits precious time with his children that he'll never get back. Your son or daughter isn't going to be around forever. Matter of fact, one day they'll be so busy with their lives that you'll have to "take a number and get in line" just to see them. Those are the unfortunate facts of life. So in the meantime, take advantage of these precious moments. If you need to, leave the cell phone back in the hotel room if it's that big of a distraction. **True rest is free of energy drains.** Remember our story in Mark 6: Jesus pinpointed the source of the disciples' fatigue, and He wisely removed it. They didn't need to feel the burden to include others. They needed time away from the very people whom they wanted to help so that they could recharge their proverbial batteries. People don't need you every moment of every day. People can't have you every moment of every day, unless of course, you have boundary issues. Good thing we tackle that very issue right now.

---

1. Dane, Kane. "The Ice Warnings Received by *Titanic*." June 17, 2019, www.titanic-titanic.com.
2. National Archives and Records Administration. "Exhibit: *Titanic* Memorandum." Updated April 15, 1998, http://www.archives.gov/exhibits/american_originals/titanic.html.
3. Peri, Camille. "10 Things to Hate about Sleep Loss." February 13, 2014, https://www.webmd.com/sleep-disorders/features/10-results-sleep-loss#1.

CHAPTER 4
BOUNDARY BACKUP

PEOPLE WILL ALWAYS NEED MORE from you, so you must learn what a healthy balance looks like. Notice the reality of what Jesus and His disciples were facing when attempting to get away and get some rest in Mark 6:33: "But many who saw them leaving recognized them and ran on foot from all the towns and got there ahead of them." People are always going to need you. Have you ever noticed that the work never runs out? That's because people's needs never end. It's in these moments when they are crying for help that you had better know the difference between a legitimate emergency and codependency.

I had a message exchange recently with a couple that I have been counseling. The wife became frustrated with her husband and became irrational and emotional. She messaged me looking for instant help. I didn't give it to her. You might be thinking, "Isn't that your job?" Well, not quite. My job is to equip people with Biblical truth; it is their job to apply the truth given. I had already given this couple the tools for spiritual success. Now it was up to them to apply it. In my message back to the wife, I told her to apply the truth

I had already given to her. That's it—nothing else! I wasn't about to rob my family of time together because someone I had already counseled wasn't applying the truth that I had given to her. That might seem harsh at first, but consider this reality: *you're either equipping people or enabling them.*

You don't have time to hold everyone's hand. You don't have time to fix everyone's problem. You can't be "all things to all people." **As demands increase, boundaries become necessary.** There's always more to do! There's always more to achieve! We often live in this never-ending cycle of exhaustion as we chase after "completion," when it doesn't exist. What do I mean by completion? It's simple. We try to make everyone happy. We extend ourselves when it's not possible to have that many friends. Come on! Those 2,835 friends on Facebook aren't really all your friends. Be honest. It's more of a status thing than it is a friendship thing. More is better until it isn't. We love to feel needed or we base our own self-value on our accomplishments; all the while, we are on a path toward burnout as depression is beginning to set in. With the instant gratification culture that we live in, we fear "not coming through" when someone "needs" us. The sad fact is that they often don't need us; they want us. We tend not to see the difference, or when we do, we're too insecure to have healthy boundaries. Why? Because we want to be wanted. So badly in fact, that we'll sacrifice our own health for it. The reality is that life is not going to simplify on its own. We must have a strategy to survive. After much thought, I have come up with this plan that works for me. I hope it helps.

Do you have a family? Do you one day aspire to have a family? If you answered "yes" to either of those questions, you better form boundaries for their sake. Remember what the Apostle Paul said to the Corinthian church in 1

Corinthians 13:1: "If I speak in the tongues of men or of angels, but do not have love, I am only a resounding gong or a clanging cymbal." In the previous chapter, the Corinthians had been fighting over prominence based on their abilities to exercise certain spiritual gifts. Paul reminds them here that it doesn't matter at all how talented or successful they are if they don't truly love others. That reality has become profound in my life. It reminds me that talent, achievements, and accolades come second to relationships. It's extremely possible that I could be achieving great things in my career with many people following me, yet I'm still a failure. Paul continues in the same passage with more evidence in 1 Corinthians 13:2-3:

> "If I have the gift of prophecy and can fathom all mysteries and all knowledge, and if I have a faith that can move mountains, but do not have love, I am nothing. If I give all I possess to the poor and give over my body to hardship that I may boast, but do not have love, I gain nothing."

Personal achievements and accolades never take the place of true Biblical love. True Biblical love is never possible without healthy boundaries. Stop cheating your family. I have found that boundaries and rest go hand-in-hand. Matter of fact, when you have boundaries in place, you set yourself up to have the healthiest relationships possible. You stop enabling people by being their crutch, and you make yourself available for the most important relational moments in your life. Here are some personal boundaries for me that I hope will help you:

1.) Three nights on, four nights off. Protect your evenings as much as possible. Maybe you work a second or third shift. Well, the point is that whatever your schedule is when you're off, be off. Over the years I've learned to make sure that I am home more than I am away. As a pastor that can be challenging. I constantly have preaching opportunities, counseling needs, leadership appointments, budget meetings, etc. I think you get the point. There is no shortage of opportunities for me to be away from home. Your life is probably the same way. You're busy. You better take control of "busy" before it takes control of you. Be intentional. Come up with a plan. Talk to your spouse about it. Here is a free commercial. I share this with almost all the couples I counsel. Sit down at the beginning of the week and talk about three things for the week: *your finances, your schedules,* and *your expectations for each other and the family.* When you do this, you position yourself to live with boundaries. You will come up with "good" compromises that meet the needs of both of you while creating a strong line of communication. More about this later.

A major reason I want to be home more than I am away is that I'm going to get only one shot to raise my kids in healthy balance. In a given week, I am home enough for family dinner, family devotions, personal conversations with each kid, assistance with homework, and some fun around the basement ping pong table. I don't want my kids to say someday that they hardly saw their dad. He was never around. He was out trying to "fix" everyone else's problems while ignoring my needs. Ouch! That can't be my legacy. That can't be your legacy. If you're presently building your earthly kingdom while ignoring your family, change right now! I mean now! Sometimes, I've literally had to tell people that I couldn't meet with them until another day. That's difficult to do, especially if you have a people-pleasing personality. The reality is that most of the time people can wait. There's only so much of you to give out to people. Make sure that your family gets the best part.

A significant moment in my life that took place when I was a senior in high school reinforced my sensitivity to family memories. I must start off by saying that the single greatest influence in my life has been my father. Without my father, I wouldn't be the man that I am today. He taught me work ethic, integrity, character, honesty, and holiness. I never heard my dad swear. Never! He wasn't perfect, but he was the embodiment of Jesus in my life. I'm serious! I wouldn't be half the man that I am today without his profound influence in my life. Now that I have made that abundantly clear, something happened that helped to shape my view of boundaries.

It was a home game—one of my last as a high school senior baseball player. Baseball was my sport. I learned it from a young age and played on an organized team every year from third grade into college. It was windy and overcast that day. I came to the plate and swung at a fastball right down the heart of the plate. The ball flew off my bat getting caught up into the strong wind that day and carried over the fence for a home run. That was the only home run I hit in high school. Matter of fact, it was the only home run over a fence that I ever hit. It wasn't that I couldn't hit; I always hit for a high average, but I didn't have much power. It was my one shining moment of hitting a home run over a fence, and my dad wasn't there. That day he got caught up in work and was late to my game. He missed it. Honestly, I don't blame him, but I know that it really bothered him for a long time. He vowed to never let that happen again, and he kept his word for the remainder of my high school career and all of my younger sister's and younger brother's careers. Do you know who else benefited that day without even realizing it? My kids.

I vowed when I became a parent to be there for my kids. My two daughters are very musical. They both play multiple instruments and are involved in the concert band in their high school. I go to their band concerts. I'm not musical, and high school band music is not exactly my favorite style of music. It's not about me; it's about them. I love them; therefore, I support what they care about. As a proud father I go, and I even make them take embarrassing pictures afterwards. My son plays soccer. It's his passion. In his last two years of high school soccer I missed one game (a make-up game) out of 43. Listen, with my three kids I didn't want to have a "home run" experience like my dad. Life is short. Set boundaries. Work will always be there. Career will always be there. Your family is growing up before your eyes. I was there to watch my son hoist district trophies, regional trophies, and a state title trophy in the air. I was there to see him score the game-winning goal in his senior year homecoming game. I was there to wipe away the tears in difficult losses. I was there through it all. I have no regrets either. I postponed meetings. I had people speak for me. I rescheduled counseling appointments so that I could be there for my kids. If I had it to do over again, I'd do the exact same thing. Be with your family more than you are away from your family. You're not going to get those moments back. That day my dad missed my home run made an important impression on me. I was not going to miss those moments in my kids' lives, and by God's grace, I've been there for every significant one. Realize that your family is your number one ministry. They must come first. You'll have a greater influence in their lives if they know that you genuinely love them supremely over all others outside your Lord Jesus Christ. I still live by that boundary: three nights on, four nights off. That boundary, however, works only if you apply my next boundary.

You can't be all things to all people at all times of the day. My second boundary is: *2.) I'm not accessible every moment of every day.* Do you ever feel as though everyone is vying for your attention? Do you ever feel guilty if you don't give it to them? When I first started in ministry, if someone called me, I'd call him back immediately. If someone needed me, at a moment's notice, I'd drop what I was doing and help them. Sometimes that's necessary. If someone is suicidal, that's worthy of immediate attention. The problem is that most times a person's "needs" are more accurately defined as his "wants." In other words, most things can wait. I used to think I was letting people down if I didn't instantly respond. I don't feel that way anymore. The fact is that a lot of people need me. It's time for all of us to prioritize.

Crisis is a funny word. Each person has a different definition of it. The actual definition from the Merriam-Webster dictionary reads: "An unstable or crucial time or state of affairs in which a decisive change is impending, especially one with the distinct possibility of a highly undesirable outcome."[1] What that means is that impending devastation is either coming or is already here. This demands immediate attention. In most cases, the "issues" that people have do not demand your immediate attention. You have probably created systems and procedures at work that, if followed, will answer their concerns. It's likely that their emotion has taken over, and they believe that they need immediate assistance. It's like when my youngest daughter came to me years ago with a splinter of wood in her finger. She was bawling as if it were the end of the world. She was looking for immediate relief. It actually became kind of a funny experience because every time I tried to use a small needle to get the splinter out, she'd pull away screaming as if I were using a chainsaw to cut her arm off. You could say that she was overreacting just a bit. It's the same thing that people tend to do. They overreact. Now, think about it for a moment: If I sent my daughter to bed with the splinter in her finger, would she actually die? Of course not. Would she still be experiencing some pain? Sure, but it wouldn't be the end of the world. Now I know what you're thinking. You wouldn't let her go to sleep like that, so you shouldn't wait until the next day to help that person in pain. Well, that's where I want to teach you. The fact is that had she calmed down, she would have been fully capable of taking the splinter out of her finger herself. Most times if people would calm down, they'd realize that they are capable of applying the truth that's already been given to them from a pastor, teacher, mentor, or life-coach. The tools are there; they simply need to be applied.

It's important that we don't become guilty of enabling people. Give them the tools necessary to succeed in the family, workplace, church, etc., and then expect them to apply them. Why? Because you can't be all things to all people. You will become emotionally and physically exhausted if you try. Do you know who suffers when you have overextended yourself? If you answered yourself, you're only partially right. You will also be stealing precious time from your family. One of the things that I have learned over the years is that people need to trust in God, not me. It's so easy as a pastor to "play God" without even realizing it. Sometimes you have to take a step back and force people to trust in God. Sometimes by making yourself unavailable you're making God available. If we truly believe the power is in the Word of God and not in our personalities, we will give people the Biblical tools and take a step back. The fact is that if you're always available to people in their "crisis" moments, then they'll never learn to stretch their faith and rely on God. The Bible doesn't say, "Trust in John Scally with all of your heart..." It surely doesn't say, "In all your ways acknowledge John Scally, and he shall direct your paths." Sure, I understand that God uses people to equip other people for ministry. It's also true that God uses mentors, life-coaches, and especially pastors to teach people truth. But don't confuse a guide for God. Jesus is the one who saves; the Holy Spirit is the one who convicts and guides; God the Father is the one who loves us with an everlasting love! Stop crippling people in their spiritual development by playing God in their lives. One day you might not be in their lives. Then what? Was their faith built on you or on God? Was their confidence in your eloquent words or in the life-changing message of the Gospel? Was their commitment based on a relationship with you or on a relationship with the almighty, never-changing, always-caring Creator?

Here are a couple practical ways to eliminate 24/7 accessibility: **(1) When you're home, be home.** Don't take phone calls or text messages. You can always listen to a voicemail when the kids have gone to bed to determine how urgent the message is. I'd even encourage you to put your phone on your dresser, refrigerator, or somewhere else that won't become a source of temptation. If you can't hear the ring or feel the buzz, you won't be curious enough to respond. **(2) Have a time boundary.** In other words, determine when "too late is too late." People have this uncanny ability to lose all social skills in this area. When someone contacts me between 5:00 and 6:00 PM, I suspect that maybe they think I don't need to eat dinner. Now, I know I could be acting a little cynical in saying that, but if you don't "put a cap" on your availability, no one else will. By the way, use common sense and get off of social media in the evening as much as possible. If people see you on Facebook, Twitter, or Instagram, they're going to consider you "available." Less screen time equals more people time.

Now, for my third major boundary: *(3) My family comes first.* You've already heard me talk extensively about my kids. I made a commitment a long time ago that I would be involved in their lives. I wouldn't miss very many of their special extracurricular events. We would eat dinner together as a family most nights. I would take the time to share the Word of God with them on a regular basis in family devotions. All of those things I have prioritized in our family. The one area that I didn't prioritize, at least early on, was my marriage. I think the reason I fell short in this area is that it's so easy to get consumed with the exhilaration of a career. Many of us have been guilty of it. Sometimes we tend to believe that the busier we are, the more successful we are. Do more "stuff." I grew up thinking more is better. I think it's a guy thing. Apply it to man's best friend—no, not a dog, but food. If you'd ask me even to this day if I'd rather have an all-you-can-eat pizza buffet or a couple of really good slices of pizza, I'm probably still picking the buffet. Why? Because more is better. I know, I know, some of you are thinking I'm disgusting. I get it, I really do. My wife for sure is thinking it too. But, it's true. Most guys would pick quantity over quality. I'm not totally sure why that is, but I do think it has something to do with a guy's thirst for more.

I still remember the day that I drove into the great metropolis of Goodells, Michigan—I say that a bit facetiously. It is actually a tiny town you might miss altogether while heading east toward Port Huron, Michigan. At the time, Goodells had a town convenience store, and that was about it. Being a city kid, I had never seen cows before until Goodells. It was my first youth pastorate after college. I joined a church of roughly 75 people, and for the first time in my life, I was Pastor John. It didn't take much time for me to throw myself into the job. I was really excited, and my excitement evidenced itself in how busy I was. The church was eager for an exciting youth ministry, and I was ready to oblige. I started van routes to pick up kids. I ran weekly activities. I became the AWANA co-director. I organized trips, Sunday evening activities, and much more. I also made connection with the teens and guys by playing modified softball, floor hockey, and roller hockey. My life was filled to the brim. The one thing I didn't mention is that I wasn't yet married. Tami and I were dating, but we weren't married. I was living the Apostle Paul's words in 1 Corinthians 7:8: "Now to the unmarried and the widows I say: It is good for them to stay unmarried, as I do." The Apostle Paul realized that as a single man he could do more for God because of the obvious reality of having less responsibility. Notice the comparison he gives in 1 Corinthians 7:32-33:

> "I would like you to be free from concern. An unmarried man is concerned about the Lord's affairs—how he can please the Lord. But a married man is concerned about the affairs of this world—how he can please his wife."

Of course, Paul wasn't saying that if you're married you can't serve the Lord. His point is that the single person has more time to serve the Lord. He doesn't have the responsibilities of caring for a family. Because I didn't have a family, it became the busiest time of my life. "Run, run, run!" became my mantra.

Then I got married. After three years of being a single youth pastor, I "tied the knot." That was a shock to both of our systems. Right before I got married, one of the men in our church told me something that I'll never forget. Since that day, I have used his wisdom over and over again in marital counseling. A man by the name of Barry looked me square in the face and told me that it was going to take me ten years before I learned how to love my wife. I thought to myself, that's "crazy talk" because I'm already in love (insert romantic wink). My mistake is that I equated love to romance, not sacrifice. Wow! I'm not totally sure on the exact timing of that prediction, but he was basically right. When I married Tami, my weekly schedule included bus routes on Sunday, teaching Sunday School, running Junior Church, having bi-weekly Sunday PM activities, working a full day Monday, visiting new families on Monday evening, working a full day on Tuesday, running our AWANA program on Tuesday evening, working a full day on Wednesday, running our Youth program on Wednesday evening, working a full day on Thursday, working a full day on Friday, playing floor hockey on Friday evening, and then either bi-weekly Saturday activities or bus visitation. I ignorantly and destructively threw my wife into that whirlwind of a lifestyle that was neither holy nor wise. The problem was that I was twenty-five years old and hard-headed. I just expected my wife to adapt to my reckless schedule. It was far from restful, and I think that it gave Tami instant anxiety before she even attempted to satisfactorily live it.

The early years of my marriage were rough. I will not attempt to "sugarcoat" it. We argued a lot. We rarely could see "eye to eye." It was not uncommon for my wife to be in tears while I was fuming in anger. I had a disease that had overcome me called "young man's disease," a.k.a selfishness. I was selfish at a high level, and the craziest thing was that I actually used the ministry to justify it. In my mind, I was expected to provide for my wife, and I wrongly equated that to financial and physical provision alone. I didn't have the ability to "listen to her heart." Oh, I could hear her, but I wasn't a good listener. Why was that? It's because I had the "noise" of everything else in my life coming in loud and clear, and there was little room for her. There was little extra time and no energy left. As a result, she would get depressed, and I would get frustrated. I needed to find balance in my life. I was anything but balanced. I needed the following strategy in James 1:19-20,

> "My dear brothers and sisters, take note of this: Everyone should be quick to listen, slow to speak and slow to become angry, because human anger does not produce the righteousness that God desires."

Hearing with the intention to make a good change is the key. If I would have been actually listening to the Word of God in my life at the time, I would have been a better listener to my wife in the early years of our marriage. Instead, I worked hard "doing" ministry without "being" what God wanted me to be. I needed someone besides my wife to tell me that I was doing too much. No one was willing to do that. The result was that I often got angry and frustrated when my wife tried to share her concerns. I was too busy to give her what she needed the most. I was too blind to see that I was actually sinning by neglecting her needs.

Your wife needs more than your physical presence. She needs you. That sounds like a contradiction until you really process it in your mind. What she needs is a husband who is able to give to her the same passion (or even greater) that he is presently giving to his career. Ouch! That probably hurts a lot of us guys. Why? Because we are achievers by nature, and it's so easy to give our spouse the crumbs of what's left over. For example, how many of us have been guilty of throwing together an anniversary dinner and gift at the last minute because we've been too busy at work? I stand guilty. It doesn't end there either. Let's be honest—it's actually easier to give our kids more than we give our spouse. If you're not careful, your wife will end up in third place this next week behind your company's merger and Junior's soccer tournament, and it's your anniversary! Oh boy, that "ain't" good! Even correcting your grammar isn't getting you out of this predicament! How does this happen? It happens when we slowly forget that the #1 person in our lives should be our spouse. The Bible describes in Genesis that the husband and wife become "one flesh" in marriage (Genesis 2:24). In other words, the two become one. Listen to me, the Bible doesn't say that you become one with your career or even your kids. A good thing can become a bad thing when it's not the best thing! There are only so many hours in a day, week, month, and year. What I found is that I was struggling in my marriage because I was giving "premium time" to everything else, thinking that our marriage would be fine with what was left over. I was wrong. It took me years to correct this trend. Be wise, and correct it now!

The same challenge is true for wives. Your husband needs your encouragement and support. You should be his biggest cheerleader. If your career is getting in the way of your marriage, you need to reassess your life. There's no amount of income that is worth enduring a struggling marriage. As I conclude this chapter, let me make it simple: Men need to be stronger emotional providers for their wives, and women need to be stronger supporters of their husbands. There is so much more I could say, but this isn't a book exclusively on marriage. Maybe I'll write that next. Until then, strengthen your marriage by having healthy boundaries as you prioritize the greatest earthly gift that you've ever received.

---

1. "Crisis." *Merriam-Webster.com Dictionary,* Merriam-Webster, https://www.merriam-webster.com/dictionary/crisis. Accessed May 18, 2023.

CHAPTER 5
CALLING AN AUDIBLE

ONE OF THE most exciting times of the year for me personally is the fall. I'm actually not a big fan of the sweltering heat of summer like most people. I enjoy the cooler temperatures of autumn. I look forward to the changing of the leaves, the weekend trips to apple orchards, and the warm and savory smells of homemade apple crisp. My birthday is also in October, and who doesn't like "free" candy at Halloween? It is also the time of year when football starts. Being a huge college football fan, I take in as much as I can get, like children scattering in a field on an Easter egg hunt. I love it! I love football. I love college football. I look forward to most Saturday afternoons when the games are played.

Did you know that football is a very organized game? You can't simply step onto the field and play. You must learn techniques. You must learn plays. You must learn to play together as one unit. Eleven players on offense, defense, or special teams working together as one. It's complicated. It's complex. It's very demanding. There are some teams whose playbooks are more than 100 pages. It was believed that the playbook of former Louisiana State University coach Les Miles was 480 pages. What you need to know is that football is not a "fly by the seat of your pants" operation. Great organization, preparation, and philosophy must be instilled into a team before it attempts to execute its playbook.

Like everything else in life, sometimes things change. Sometimes you are called upon to be flexible. In other words, sometimes you have to deviate from the planned moment into something more spontaneous. In football, we call that an audible. It's when the quarterback brings his team to the line of scrimmage, and he realizes that the play that was originally called is not going to work. He assesses the defense that he is facing, and he changes plays at the line of scrimmage. It's not easy to call an audible. Everyone must be fully focused when he does so, or the play isn't going to work. Worse yet, someone could get hurt. For instance, if the offensive line, who is supposed to protect the quarterback, thought it was a passing play when it's now a running play, the protection will not be there, and the quarterback could get blindsided. We call that a breakdown in communication. Communication breakdowns only happen to teams who are not fully focused on one another. Communication breakdowns happen only to teams on which the players are more focused on themselves than they are on the team. When a team is used to working together, they respond to challenging circumstances in successful ways. **Flexibility is possible when the culture is stable.**

Remember our previous story of "prepared rest" that Jesus had planned for his disciples. They had been so busy preaching and teaching and impacting people that they didn't even have structured time to eat. Jesus decided that they'd go to a solitary place to rest and recharge. Then he called an audible. Mark 6:32-34 says,

> "So they went away by themselves in a boat to a solitary place. But many who saw them leaving recognized them and ran on foot from all the towns and got there ahead of them. When Jesus landed and saw a large crowd, he had compassion on them, because they were like sheep without a shepherd. So he began teaching them many things."

This might seem like a contradiction to what I previously said about boundaries, but it isn't. Remember, there are unique times when people will need you, and you'll have to respond. These moments are the exception, not the norm. When Jesus got off the boat and saw the crowds, he became emotional. He determined this to be a moment when he needed to be flexible, to the point of abandoning his original plan for rest. Why? Because he saw them as helpless sheep walking toward disaster without a shepherd. I personally believe that people were saved from their sin that day. There will be times when you'll have to rely on supernatural strength and energy to do the will of God. Remember, this can't be the norm in your life. If it is, you will soon "burn out."

Teamwork is essential to Christian influence. Does God need us to do his will? The answer is clearly no. Does God want to use us to do his will? The answer is an emphatic yes! If you look at 1 Corinthians 12, you see that all believers in Jesus have necessary roles on his team. Think of it this way: If you had to give up one of your five senses, what would it be? Which one is nonessential to your life? I've thought through this before, and at first I thought it would be easy, then I realized it wasn't! It went something like this. Maybe I can give up my sense of smell. Oh wait, then I wouldn't be able to smell that aroma from the lasagna my grandma prepared with the sausage covered in sauce. Or, worse yet, I wouldn't be able to smell the fragrance of my wife. Instead, maybe I could give up taste. Then, I realized that there was no way I'd want to give up the taste of an ice-cold Pepsi going down my throat on a hot summer's day. What about touch? Well, that's not even an option! I'll never forget holding my kids when they were first born or the embrace of my wife after returning from a conference or a missions trip. What about sight? Can you imagine never being able to see the sunrise and sunset? Can you imagine never being able to see a snow-covered mountain or fall's magnificent colors? Never mind that men are driven by sight. If I could never see the beauty of my wife again, that would be devastating to my life. That leaves hearing. Out of all of the senses, this is the one that I thought I could give up the quickest. That is until I began to think of the things that I would be missing, like the sound of laughter at the dinner table or the thrill of the crowd at a ball game. I was recently sitting at the dinner table with my family just listening to the silliness and laughter. Hearing the stories and the jokes brought a smile to my face. I remember earlier this year when my son's soccer team defeated their Catholic rival in soccer. When his team scored to take a lead that they would never give up, the crowd erupted! I can't imagine being there and not being able to hear the thrill of the crowd.

    The lesson I learned is that God created the human body to need all five senses. Each sense is indispensable. Each sense has such a unique function that one depends on the other. That is the reality in 1 Corinthians 12. Notice some of the Apostle Paul's strong words in describing the teamwork of the church. He uses the unity of the human body to make his point. Notice his reminder to the church in 1 Corinthians 12:15-20:

> "Now if the foot should say, 'Because I am not a hand, I do not belong to the body,' it would not for that reason stop being part of the body. And if the ear should say, 'Because I am not an eye, I do not belong to the body,' it would not for that reason stop being part of the body. If the whole body were an eye, where would the sense of hearing be? If the whole body were an ear, where would the sense of smell be? But in fact God has placed the parts in the body, every one of them, just as he wanted them to be. If they were all one part, where would the body be? As it is, there are many parts, but one body."

We all have a role to play in God's church. The sooner you embrace your purpose through your spiritual gifts, the more joy you will experience. Remember the words of Mark Twain: "The two greatest days of your life are the day you were born and the day you find out why." Of course, truly the greatest day of your life is the day you called upon Jesus to save you from your sin, believing on him as your Lord and Savior! At the moment of salvation, your purpose began!

What does this have to do with rest? I'll get there in a minute or two. Back to our story. Remember, Jesus had decided to call an audible and care for the people in need. Part of the greatness of Jesus as master-teacher is that not only did he teach those who needed to hear truth, but he also involved his disciples in the process. They were a part of his team. They were not there to simply be spectators;

they were there to be participators. After Jesus had taught the people all day, it was time to go home. The problem was that many of them were far away from their homes, and it was time for dinner. Jesus' disciples saw this as a problem; Jesus saw this as an opportunity.

Instead of sending the people home hungry, Jesus decided to show his power to the large crowd including his disciples. He told his disciples to "figure out how to feed the people." The problem was that the crowd was over 5,000 men and probably well over 15,000 people (Mark 6:44). There were no McDonald's or Taco Bell fast food restaurants back in the day. They weren't going to send Peter with the church van to pick up some value meals and 10-packs of tacos. Matter of fact, it would have taken them about eight months of a man's wages (Mark 6:37) to pay for all of this food. It was impossible! Except it wasn't, because Jesus was there! Remember that nothing is impossible in your life when you are in the will of God! So, Jesus told his disciples to go and get whatever food they could find in the crowd. They came back with five loaves of bread and two fishes (Mark 6:38). Remember that little is much with Jesus. So, Jesus had his disciples put the people into groups (Mark 6:39-40). He then proceeded to bless the food and hand it to his disciples to pass out (Mark 6:41-42). In that moment, Jesus multiplied the food so that everyone could eat. It was a miracle that they saw with their own eyes. Don't miss an often overlooked part of the story: he used his disciples in the process. They were extremely important to the team. They helped to make sure all of the people were cared for, having just received the life-changing words of Jesus. What a day! Was it worth it to delay their vacation?

Sometimes, in extreme situations, rest has to be delayed. Again, this is the exception to the rule. The reason

I am sharing this principle is that there can be real tension between "boundary issues" and "not wanting to be stretched." God is in the "stretching business!" He is looking to do great things in your life as long as you are obedient to his Word. You should always be willing to create a backup plan for extra rest when duty unexpectedly calls. Jesus taught the people about lasting contentment and purpose in kingdom living. That day changed their lives! That day changed his disciples' lives too. He engaged them in the process of experiencing the miracle for themselves. **The miracle of the moment happens when you're willing to be stretched.** Jesus stretched his disciples' physical stamina and spiritual awareness, but Jesus did so with a planned "rest stop ahead!"

When the quarterback decides to change the play at the line of scrimmage, will you be prepared? Are you even paying attention? This book is all about rest, but let's be honest. You don't even need this book if you're not passionately living life. We are meant to be achievers for the glory of God. Do you know what's worse than having too much passion? It's having no passion at all. You are a part of the greatest team ever assembled—God's team, the church! We are meant to serve God and others with a sacrificial heart. Don't use laziness as an excuse! This book is not meant to motivate you to go buy yourself a La-Z-Boy chair while someone feeds you bonbons on a perpetual vacation. Instead, it's meant to give you balance so that your life can be maximized for the glory of God! One of the most gratifying feelings, which has become commonplace in my life, is the feeling of exhaustion by the time Friday comes. Do you know what comes after Friday? No, it's not Saturday—It's my day off! I guard it. I protect it. Only God can change it! Sometimes he does, but it's rare!

CHAPTER 6
STOPPING A TREND

I think we would all agree that society as a whole is too busy. As I mentioned earlier in the book, at times I've found myself too busy to eat lunch or even use the bathroom. I'm not the exception. I'm the norm. We have an innate desire to achieve. Because of that insatiable drive, we often are willing to cut corners when it comes to our health if it means "getting ahead." We've all been guilty of it until we have no choice but to rest. Sometimes that's a nervous breakdown; sometimes that's a pandemic.

I was so excited. My wife and I were on our way to Orlando, Florida, for the Exponential Conference on church growth. I couldn't wait to sit in the breakout sessions on multi-site ministry since that has become the vision for our church moving forward. We were leaving snowy Flint, Michigan, for sunny Orlando, Florida. Who wouldn't be excited? We were also staying with some of our dear friends who recently moved from Tennessee to Orlando. It was going to be an amazing week!

After the conference was over at mid-week, we went to Disney World for a couple of days. Our Orlando friends had purchased season passes, and they were so excited to show us the newest experiences and rides in the parks. The one excursion that became the highlight for my wife and me was the Star Wars experience. I'll never forget entering "Galaxy's Edge" and experiencing "The Rise of the Resistance" in Hollywood Studios. Talk about adrenaline and excitement as you enter the "Death Star" and you're surrounded by a hundred Stormtroopers. It was simply amazing and breathtaking! It wasn't the only incredible experience we had either. All day, and the next day as well, we raced from ride to ride trying to get the full Disney experience. By the end of each day we were fully exhausted, having experienced vacation at its highest level. Or…had we?

Have you ever heard the phrase "I need a vacation after my vacation!"? If we're completely honest, the fact is that *even on vacation* there is little rest. My wife is the biggest culprit. Yes, I'm calling her out. No, I will not admit to this if you tell her! I guess it's in writing, so I'm sunk! Anyway, when we are on a family vacation, it is a race against time. It is exactly what I previously mentioned. We have to get the "full experience!" After all, we are paying for this! "Get out of bed, John!" I can hear those words ringing in my ears even now! I remember on one occasion when it was really evident. We were at Disney World (Can you see a pattern here?) when my wife decided that we needed to take advantage of our "magic hours," meaning the extra time before and after the park closes. In other words, for those who stay in a Disney resort, they are able to get to the park earlier and stay later than the average person. So, my wife was up at 5:30 AM—*on vacation*—to go to the park with my daughters. My son and I held our ground and didn't get out of bed until 8:00 AM. What did that cost us? Well, the girls sent us pictures of the biggest cinnamon-drenched elephant ears we have ever seen. Was it worth it to stay in bed? You decide. The point is that even on our vacations we're not getting much rest.

Just like our family vacations, my wife and I came back from that conference in Orlando exhausted. We were up early in the morning every day, and we didn't get to bed until late each night. We came home tired and somewhat sick. Then, it happened. In a matter of a couple of days, the whole world changed. Coronavirus, or COVID-19, caused our world to come to a screeching halt. I will never forget the moment when it hit me that we wouldn't be gathering as a church for a while. Honestly, I fought that idea for a while. In the beginning, as other churches were pulling back, I arrogantly told our church that "nothing would be changing—business as usual." God humbled me. We were done. Let's be honest, none of us were ready for such a shock to our systems. We were used to ballgames, concerts, plays, school, work, dinners out, parties, church, and sometimes even more in the same week or even day. We were consumed with being busy, like a drug that we had to have. We even talked ourselves into believing that busy meant dedicated; busy meant committed; busy meant success.

Entering the "stay-at-home" order from our governor in Michigan really reshaped my thinking. It caused me to take inventory of my life. What is really important? What really matters? I found myself realizing that I was way too consumed with watching sports. Am I going to remove watching sports from my life when they come back? No, but I will probably watch them less. Why is that? Because my appreciation for what truly matters has grown since the pandemic. I sat at the dinner table the other day overwhelmed with a sense of gratitude as I heard my kids laughing and teasing each other. I had nowhere to go and nothing to do. I wasn't trying to rush through dinner to get to Wednesday night Bible study or Thursday night Celebrate Recovery. I was forced to rest, even while eating dinner. What an amazing experience it was. Since the pandemic, I have heard of many other similar stories. Families eating dinner together for the first time in years. Families playing board games together for the first time in years. Families taking walks or riding bikes together for the first time in a long time. Families have reengaged. While I miss my Red Wings hockey and a good steak from Lucky's in Davison, Michigan, I now realize that a "break in action" was exactly what most of us truly needed.

It will be interesting to see what most people do when the pandemic is over. Maybe it's already over as you're reading this book. How has it changed your life for the better? Have you made some adjustments, or have you slowly jumped back into the chaos of restlessness? I hope we can learn from history, or else we're doomed to repeat it. How can we stop this trend of restlessness? We'll tackle this challenge in the forms of personal demand, spiritual nourishment, and important foundations.

Number one: **Make rest a non-negotiable part of your life.** Let's go back to Jesus' example in Mark 6. After Jesus had stretched his disciples' faith, he made sure that they received some badly needed rest. There's a small but important detail that we cannot afford to miss in the text. Verse 45 reads, "Immediately **Jesus made his disciples get into the boat** and go on ahead of him to Bethsaida, **while** he dismissed the crowd." Jesus acted selflessly by sending the disciples on "vacation" while he finished the job. He did not want them engaged or distracted any further. He acted swiftly. He saw this moment as a non-negotiable moment.

Isn't it really easy to make excuses when it comes to rest? We tell ourselves that we "have" to stay up later, work longer, or push harder. It reminds me of a teenager pushing the limits. If you tell him to be home at midnight, he's going to push it to 12:15 AM or even later. It is intrinsically part of who we are as people. We always think we can accomplish a little bit more, so we push ourselves. Sometimes that's a good thing. Many times that can be detrimental to our health. What should we do? **Prioritize rest the same way that you prioritize production.**

One thing that I found over the years is that if I am well rested I can actually achieve more. For example, my sermon preparation day is Wednesday. Sometimes in anticipation of writing my sermon I begin working on it Tuesday to get ahead so that it's easier for me on Wednesday. Here's the issue: I was staying up later than usual on Tuesday to "get ahead" which led to the sacrifice of quality on Wednesday because I was overtired. I quickly realized that it wasn't worth it. One word that you need to write down, star, circle, and mark with a highlighter is the word *efficient*. The Merriam-Webster dictionary defines *efficient* in this way: "productive of desired effects; especially capable of producing desired results with little or no waste (as of time or materials)." More time doesn't always equal better results. Sometimes it equals the same or less results because we're not focused on the task at hand. You are made to achieve! It's in our purpose. We naturally desire to be successful moms, husbands, bosses, friends, leaders, etc. Therefore, we read books, we practice, we watch YouTube, we go to Bible studies and seminars, we listen to podcasts, we take in advice from trusted mentors, and so much more. **We prioritize growth, but it's all for naught if we're not in the proper frame of mind, and we won't be in the proper frame of mind if we're not rested.** Notice the wisdom of Solomon in Psalm 127:2: "In vain you **rise early and stay up late**, toiling for food to eat – for he grants sleep to those he loves." The mistake the author highlights is what's called "artificial lengthening." We tend to think that we can "beat the system" or "stretch the day," but in reality all we're doing is diminishing the quality of what we're trying to achieve. I have learned the hard way in this area. I no longer try to stretch out the day like I once did. Instead, I get proper rest so that I can achieve at a high level. The goal is never simply completion. Anyone can complete a job. The goal has to be excellence. It's the truly great leaders who understand that excellence comes from efficiency, and efficiency comes from a healthy mindset. I've noticed that when I'm truly rested, my sermon preparation is much richer. Stop believing the lie that you have to trade rest for effectiveness. They are meant to go together. Commit to rest and watch your production level—no matter what you do for a living—explode in growth! That's going to happen only when you are determined to make rest a non-negotiable part of your life.

Number two: **Begin to see spiritual rest as a vital part of your life.** One aspect of rest that often gets overlooked is spiritual rest. We can be so busy doing ministry that we forget to spend time with the object of that ministry, our Savior. I often tell our church that we must have spiritual balance in our lives, meaning that we take in and we give out. Let's be honest, most Christians are out of balance in one aspect or the other. You have the crowd of people who are fixated with information. These people are at every gathering, class, and study the church offers. They have a great deal of biblical information, but they don't know what to do with all of it. Then, there's the crowd of people who are obsessed with service. They serve in the kids program, youth program, senior citizens program, the community outreach, the blood drive, the ladies missionary ministry, and the "doggie blessing day" at church. Okay, that last one is the Methodists, scratch that one. Come on, it's a joke. You get the point though. They are consumed with giving, serving, and loving. Both styles are sincere commitments, but both are sincerely wrong without the other. We are called to balance. Remember the growth process of Jesus that we already talked about in Luke 2:52: "And Jesus grew in wisdom and stature, and in favor with God and man." You must find the balance. Unfortunately, the balance is usually lost in the area of spiritual rest. What do I mean?

It's not easy, but it's possible and usually probable that people eventually learn how to physically rest. What is not so probable is the spiritual rest part. Why? Because we have trust issues. What do I mean by that? What I mean is that we don't trust God the way that we should, so we're always trying to "make it happen" in our own power. That, my friends, is exhausting. It might lead to a superficial trace of success in the beginning, but in the long run, it fails. I love the fact that Jesus attached spiritual rest to physical rest. He wisely understood how intrinsically connected they are. The kind of rest that Jesus exemplified and encouraged of his disciples was grounded in prayer and in his truth. It was more than the absence of work. It was spiritual refreshment. Notice his example in Mark 6:46: "After leaving them, he went up on a mountainside to pray." Jesus was always modeling prayer and teaching his disciples how to pray (Luke 11:1-13). Spiritual renewal always involves prayer.

What makes prayer so important to spiritual rest? It's the presence of God in your life. If you have called upon Jesus to save you from your sin, you have the Holy Spirit living inside you. Let's take a quick journey through Hebrews 4 to further examine spiritual rest. Toward the end of the book, we'll take another look at this chapter. For now, realize that the book of Hebrews is all about the supremacy of Christ over all things. He is compared to the great Old Testament Jewish hero Moses. He is compared to angels. He is compared to priests. In every comparison, Jesus Christ is found to be superior to each one. There is also an amazing comparison as it relates to different types of rest. Notice the words of Hebrews 4:1-5:

> "Therefore, since the promise of entering his rest still stands, let us be careful that none of you be found to have fallen short of it. For we also have had the good news proclaimed to us, just as they did; but the message they heard was of no value to them, because they did not share the faith of those who obeyed. Now we who have believed enter that rest, just as God has said, 'So I declared an oath in my anger, "They shall never enter my rest."' And yet his works have been finished since the creation of the world. For somewhere he has spoken about the seventh day in these words: 'On the seventh day God rested from all his works.' And again in the passage above he says, 'They shall never enter my rest.'"

You're probably wondering what these Bible verses actually mean. The focus of them is comparing a past opportunity for Israel with a present opportunity for us.

Many years before these verses were written, God promised Israel that if they were fully committed to him, he would bless them with rest. This rest included peace from their enemies in the lush land of Canaan. It was a place that the Bible literally described as a "land flowing with milk and honey" (Numbers 13:27). The modern-day equivalent terminology would be "steak and pasta," at least in my Italian mind. Unfortunately, Israel rebelled against God and wandered around in the wilderness for many years missing out on God's blessing. You will always miss out on God's blessings in your life when you attempt to do things your own way! They allowed their fear to overwhelm their faith (the full story is in Numbers 13-14). Instead of focusing on the presence of God with them, they focused on the presence of "giants" in front of them.

There was a generation who missed out on the blessings of God, and you don't want to follow their example and make the same mistake. They missed out on this incredible rest because they ignored the presence of God. The "good news" was made known to them just as it has been to us. The key is our response to it as it relates to a complete trust and dependence on God, especially in challenging circumstances in which we could be tempted to trust in our own abilities. For the believer in Jesus, you and I enter that rest now. The word for "enter" is in the present tense and seems to be indicating that the rest is not limited to the future but is happening now. For the believing follower of Jesus Christ, this means that he can experience a quality of life that includes God's peace, confidence of salvation, and supernatural strength (Philippians 1:6) right now! That's pretty encouraging considering how difficult life can be. If Israel would have trusted in God's strength instead of their own perceptions, they would have been blessed with spiritual rest. How about you? Who or what are you trusting in to get you through today?

From the very beginning of time, God gave us a model of rest to follow. Have you ever accomplished something, and then you were able to reflect on your work? When God was finished with creation, there was nothing to add to or subtract from the finished product because it was perfect. The rest that we enter into through faith is unrivaled, perfect. When God finished His creation, there was the opportunity of this rest in Him. The seventh day creation rest and the promised land of Canaan rest are but "types" of the saving eternal rest Jesus Christ offers. An incredible result of this rest is grace over guilt as you live with a new vitality for life grounded in confidence in Christ!

We have to go a little further in the passage to get the full effect. Notice Hebrews 4:6-11:

> "Therefore since it still remains for some to enter that rest, and since those who formerly had the good news proclaimed to them did not go in because of their disobedience, God again set a certain day, calling it 'Today.' This he did when a long time later he spoke through David, as in the passage already quoted: 'Today, if you hear his voice, do not harden your hearts.' For if Joshua had given them rest, God would not have spoken later about another day. There remains, then, a Sabbath-rest for the people of God; for anyone who enters God's rest also rests from their works, just as God did from his. Let us, therefore, make every effort to enter that rest, so that no one will perish by following their example of disobedience."

Often, one man's failure is another man's lesson. Unbelief has severe consequences. Israel learned that the hard way. God offered rest in Moses' time and continued to offer it in David's time (Psalm 95:7-11; Exodus 17:1-7), and today he is still patiently inviting people to enter His rest. Each generation has had an opportunity to live in faith. The wilderness generation lived in disobedience and forfeited their opportunity for rest. Instead, they lived in fear, which led to regret. Spiritual rest is always grounded in trust. In my own vulnerability, I choose to believe that God is greater! He overcomes my weaknesses when I fully trust in him for his honor and glory alone.

Remember, Hebrews is all about comparisons. In every situation, Jesus reigns superior. Whatever you've been fooled into believing this world has to offer is simply inferior to Jesus. So many people are chasing after rest, or their own version of happiness. Maybe it's more money. Maybe it's a position in the company. Maybe it's a bigger house. Maybe it's a world-renowned name. Whatever it is, you won't find what you're looking for without Jesus. Even the rest of health, wealth, and prosperity pales in comparison to what Jesus offers. Notice this incredible analogy of showing the superiority of Jesus through the following question and answer. Who led the children of Israel into the Promised Land? It was Joshua who came after Moses. Did you know that the name for "Joshua" is the Hebrew form of the Greek name Jesus? So, "Jesus" led the children of Israel into the land of promise, but the writer's point is that an even greater Jesus will lead His people into an even greater rest! That rest is salvation by grace through faith in Jesus alone. In other words, Jesus is greater than "Jesus" (Joshua)!

For the Israelites, they may have thought of their rest as the time when there would be an absence of wars (Deuteronomy 25:19), but God was offering His people a greater rest...a rest for the souls of men (Matthew 11:28-30). It was a rest that was impossible to obtain by the works of man. Learn from the failures of the children of Israel, and with urgency enter into that rest now! You can have peace with God now and eternal life on a new earth later. We do not need to wait for the next life to enjoy God's rest and peace. We can have it now! Make every effort to enter that rest now. The presence of God brings the greatest rest, and that rest is found in a relationship with him grounded in prayer.

Relief is temporary; rest is satisfying. I am a big Pepsi fan. I love to drink it often. There's just something about an ice-cold glass filled with Pepsi. I actually enjoy Pepsi more than Coke because of its sweetness. It's addicting, especially on a Friday night with my favorite pizza. One thing about "pop" (I'm a Northerner.) is that it always leaves me wanting more. I remember one time when I experienced that reality as a kid. It was opening day for Little League baseball in East Detroit (now called Eastpointe), Michigan. On that special day there was an all-day parade with food. You could get as many hot dogs, chips, and pop as you wanted. So, guess what I did? I kept going up to the Pepsi stand and getting cups of Pepsi. I did it over and over and over again because I could. I was in all my glory—until I wasn't. After a few hours of all-you-can-drink carbonated sugar, my stomach began to twist and turn. The rest was history! I kept returning for more Pepsi because the satisfaction of the previous glass had worn off. It's a completely different experience with water. On a hot day after cutting the lawn, it's an ice-cold glass of water that satisfies. While I might enjoy the taste of Pepsi more, it's the glass of water that actually satisfies me. It replenishes my system and prepares me for the next challenge ahead. That's the difference between relief and rest. This world offers short-term relief. God offers long-term rest. What does that truly look like?

Jesus offers rest that requires commitment to him (Matthew 11:28-30). He gives a peace that is the byproduct of thankful prayer, not the absence of activity. The Apostle Paul's words drive home this point in Philippians 4:6-7:

> "Do not be anxious about anything, but in every situation, by prayer and petition, with thanksgiving, present your requests to God. And the peace of God, which transcends all understanding, will guard your hearts and your minds in Christ Jesus."

Notice how we are commanded to pray in thanksgiving in every situation. The reality is that when you're focused on what God has already done in your life, you're less likely to worry about the immediate challenges in front of you. In fact, you are spiritually strengthened to present your requests in a way that builds confidence in what he is going to do. I love the word picture of "guarding your hearts." Like a soldier keeping watch, God's peace will protect you from irrational thinking and behavior. Once again, spiritual rest always finds its way back to trust in God. It is satisfying at the highest level.

Let's take a minute now and talk about some of the practical byproducts of this kind of heavenly satisfaction. It's satisfaction that is a result of discipline. Let's be honest, most of life's greatest achievements are because of discipline. The Christian journey is no different. God expects us to discipline our thoughts, attitudes, and actions. **Spiritual disciplines advance enduring rest.** What does this mean? It means that in order to experience the practical byproducts of heavenly satisfaction, we must make every effort to "exercise." I'm not necessarily talking about physical exercise either, which makes many of us happy. A lot of us are like the guy who says, "I believe in fitness; fitting this whole pizza into my mouth." Let's be honest that we Americans like our carbs. So, be encouraged with the Apostle Paul's words in 1 Timothy 4:8: "For physical training is of some value, but godliness has value for all things, holding promise for both the present life and the life to come." The point that he was trying to make is that physical exercise has some value, but Godly exercise has the most value.

The Apostle Paul took this to the next level in his own life as proven in his "workout plan" in 1 Corinthians 9:24-27:

> "Do you not know that in a race all the runners run, but only one gets the prize? Run in such a way as to get the prize. Everyone who competes in the games goes into strict training. They do it to get a crown that will not last, but we do it to get a crown that will last forever. Therefore I do not run like someone running aimlessly; I do not fight like a boxer beating the air. No, I strike a blow to my body and make it my slave so that after I have preached to others, I myself will not be disqualified for the prize."

How we live our lives is just as important as what we do with our lives. We must be spiritually disciplined. The Apostle Paul did not want to be like a boxer throwing "haymakers" at the wind. Instead, he wanted to make sure that he prepared himself to honor God in all ways.

Just as a boxer must condition for a prize boxing match, all Christians must condition themselves for the spiritual fight. This involves the spiritual disciplines of Bible reading, Scripture memorization, prayer, mentorship, and service. There is nothing more satisfying than working hard and achieving something in life. Just think of how much more satisfying it will be when God blesses your life as a result of your commitment to spiritual exercise. If you don't "feel" close to God, it's probably because you're making little to no effort to incorporate spiritual disciplines into your life (James 4:8).

Number three: **Follow the pattern for success.** I love the fact that God never asks us to do something without first modeling it for us. He is a gracious father who always lays out a formula for success in front of us. As a father, you should never ask your kids to do things that are humanly impossible for them. I can think of times in my own life when I was frustrated with my kids because they didn't do what I asked them to do fast enough, strong enough, or efficiently enough. The problem wasn't them; it was me, because what I was asking them to do wasn't fair. They weren't able to fulfill my request. God will never do that to you! He always sets us up for success. It's just a matter of whether we're going to *go down his path* (Proverbs 3:5-6) for our lives.

The pattern of success that I am talking about has its roots in the beginning of creation. God created the world and all of its magnificence, and then he did something less for himself and more for us. Notice this profound moment in Genesis 2:1-3:

> "Thus the heavens and the earth were completed in all their vast array. By the seventh day God had finished the work he had been doing; so on the seventh day he rested from all his work. Then God blessed the seventh day and made it holy, because on it he rested from all the work of creating that he had done."

The word for "rest" in the Hebrew is the word *Shabbat*, meaning "to cease"—not from exhaustion but from accomplishment. God had accomplished his task. The greatest kind of rest always comes after accomplishment. We are meant to achieve; we are meant to rest after achievement. Now the difference here is that God didn't need to rest because of exhaustion; we on the other hand do. So, our rest is grounded in both reflection and physical need.

God knows that we need physical rest. He also knows that when we rest after achievement, it is the best kind of rest. There is nothing quite like resting after a long but successful week at work. In our culture, everyone knows what TGIF means. That acronym carries even more meaning to the person who has worked hard all week and now is ready to enjoy some rest on the weekend. From the beginning of time, God modeled to us a built-in system for rest. We are meant to apply it to our lives. It doesn't end with physical rest either. Matter of fact, it's just the beginning.

God not only rested on the seventh day, but he also blessed that day. What does that even mean? It means that he sanctified it, or "set it apart." It's different. It's like no other day. When I was a boy, I can remember "the day!" From the time of early adolescence, my dad would take me to Red Wings games. I told you earlier that I am a big hockey fan. All week, I would look forward to the day when my dad and I would go to these games. I counted the time down. One of my closest friends would go hunting with his dad. That was his special day to look forward to. It's pretty clear why these days meant so much to me and my friend. During the week, we both had to go to school. We both had to go to bed early. We both had to do homework. We both had to do all of the tasks that made up our responsibilities.

Let's be honest, responsibilities are not always fun—just ask my kids after they've picked up our dog's "backyard blessings!" We fulfill our responsibilities knowing that there is something awaiting us to look forward to in the near future. For me, what ultimately made those times so special was the time with my dad.

When God "set apart" the seventh day, he did so for us to worship him without distraction. He knows how busy life can be, and he wants our undivided attention. He wants time with his kids. The seventh day of creation became a model for man to follow. The Mosaic Law (Ten Commandments) that was later given to the Jewish nation (Exodus 20:8-11) demanded that this day be set apart unto the Lord for worship. In other words, the day belonged to God. This day became known as the Sabbath Day. In a practical sense, rest from ordinary labor would allow for worship and spiritual service to be the focus. We shouldn't underestimate the importance that God placed on rest. In the Ten Commandments, the command to rest is there on the same list alongside prohibitions against the heinous sins of murder, stealing, and adultery.

Many years later, God's church in the spirit of Sabbath made the first day of the week its focus for worship. Why the switch? Well, Jesus arose from the grave conquering sin and death on the first day of the week. The church adopted this day as its primary day for organized worship (Acts 20:7; 1 Corinthians 16:2). Sunday is *not* "Funday" as our culture calls it. It is worship day! It is time with our Heavenly Father and with our brothers and sisters in Christ. It's meant to be set apart unto God for selfless worship and spiritual rejuvenation. I wish I had a dollar for every person who told me after Sunday worship how encouraging it was in the moment and how motivational it was for their upcoming week. When we gather together to sing praises to our God, to hear his word preached, to give tithes and offerings for his mission, to remember his sacrifice in communion, and to witness new believers in baptism, we are "resting" in his grace. Our undivided attention is on our Creator, Savior, and Sustainer. What could be better than that? The answer is absolutely nothing!

In those moments of going to hockey games, what I found more meaningful than the actual games was uninterrupted time with my father. It was during those times when I learned from him and was encouraged by him. He is my earthly father, and he's pretty awesome! Just think about how much greater your Heavenly Father is! He has lovingly given us the pattern for spiritual success. **A successful "season" demands rest for another successful season.** You have many challenges staring you in the face come Monday morning. Make sure you're prepared for those challenges having "slowed your life down" to worship and trust your Lord God ahead of time. Your lifestyle is unsustainable if rest is not a regular part of it. What is it going to cost you? Your career? Your health? Your family? Your relationship with God? It's time to stop the trend before the trend stops you! Sometimes the greatest challenge comes in the most unexpected moments of life. Will you be ready for what's next?

CHAPTER 7
WORN OUT AFTER WINNING

I LOVE SUGAR. I love butter. I often have joked in the past that my veins are filled with sugar and butter. That's not very funny to my primary care doctor, but to this guy, it makes me smile. The other thing that I left out that's also up near the top of my "happy list" is bread. I love bread. Now sprinkle some sugar or butter on some bread, and we're in business. While we're at it, let's throw in some pasta, too. I am Italian, so what would you expect? Now, that's a glorious meal! For years, my mom would take Italian sausage and slow cook it all day in tomato sauce. By the time it was dinner, the sausage would melt in your mouth! Wow! Are you hungry yet? So, some bread, sausage, and pasta will get you a great meal. Do you know what else it will get you? A nap. Do you know why? Carbs. Talk about a meal filled with carbs. It's pretty well known that carbs cause fatigue.

Matter of fact, there are all sorts of well-known causes of fatigue that we experience. One that might come as a surprise is caffeine. Research in the field has shown that while caffeine gives an initial burst of energy, too much of it can aggravate other contributors to exhaustion and lead to worsening cravings. Like sugar, it might leave you wanting more and still fail to deliver in terms of actual energy or performance. It's also been proved that too much cell phone use before bed can create fatigue because of the melatonin/blue light effect. We already know that depression, inactivity, and stress cause fatigue.

One cause of fatigue that you will never hear about, however, is success. That's right. Success breeds fatigue if it is not handled properly. **One of the most vulnerable times in your life is after you have achieved success.** Why? It's because you have expended so much energy toward a cause that you believe in, leaving you drained and surprisingly discouraged. But, why? You achieved! You won! You succeeded! You just accomplished your goal! You just got the job! You just finished the home project! You just won the award! Well, the answer is complicated, and I intend to paint a picture in this chapter that will enlighten you to your "underrated enemy" that will cause you to be worn out.

Before we go any further, let's take a look back as we review how we've gotten to this point. We are in the middle of a "new you" focusing on finding value in prioritizing rest. From the beginning, God created it. In the Ten Commandments given to Israel, God included it. To his disciples, Jesus modeled it. From his church, God demands it. Don't let the unachievable expectations of others cause you mental and emotional fatigue. The religious leaders of Jesus' day were "good" at making people feel "bad" based on outward man-made rules. Also, forgive yourself. God forgave you. What gives you the right to do less than what God has done for you? In the last chapter we were reminded that you can't "skip out" on the basic necessities of life. If you don't have time to use the bathroom, you're too busy. We also were reminded that demands only increase, so have boundaries; also, true rest is not just the absence of activity. In other words, take the time to pray and read your Bible in solitude, growing close to the Lord. Rest matters. Don't underrate it. Now, we'll dissect how rest must follow success.

The story unfolds in 1 Kings 18-19 with the northern kingdom of Israel being led by the wicked king named Ahab and queen named Jezebel. Israel found herself in a perpetual state of idolatry worshiping false gods while rejecting the one true God. The evil duo had led Israel into worshiping the Canaanite "land fertility" god named Baal. Introduce into the story a man by the name of Elijah who was one of the last standing prophets of God. Matter of fact, his aggressive confrontation of Ahab's sinful leadership brings us to a boiling point in the story. I love the fact that Elijah cared more about the honor of God than his own well-being. It was not uncommon in those days for people who stood up against royalty to be either thrown into jail or beheaded. Elijah didn't care.

Elijah had enough of the wicked leadership of Israel. He was filled with righteous indignation over what was happening to his beloved people. Remember, everything rises and falls on leadership. Elijah wasn't the only prophet in Israel either. In fact, there were 450 prophets of the false god Baal. Talk about being out-numbered—yet it didn't stop Elijah from standing for truth. He had a passion in his soul that ignited his stand for God. Israel had been warned countless times that she was to love and worship the Lord God only. Unfortunately, it is often too easy for us to "worship other gods." Sometimes we need an Elijah in our lives to set everything back in its proper place of priority.

What happened next is one of the most incredible stories in the Bible. Elijah challenged the prophets of Baal to a "spiritual duel" to finally put to rest the question of who is the true God. The Bible tells us this in 1 Kings 18:21: "Elijah went before the people and said, 'How long will you waver between two opinions? If the Lord is God, follow him; but if Baal is God, follow him.'" Elijah told the prophets of Baal to take a bull and put it on an altar as an offering to their god. He would do the same. He then told them to pray to their god to bring down fire from heaven to consume the sacrifice. He would do the same. He declared in front of these false prophets that whoever answers the prayers is the one true God.

Think about the scene. Think about the challenge. Imagine thousands of people gathering out of curiosity to see what was going to happen. It's like when you were in junior high, and you heard someone yell "fight!" down the hallway. Everyone came running, including you, to see what was going to happen. Here is Elijah; he is the minority. All of these assembled people had either been worshiping Baal or leading worship to Baal. Can you imagine the pressure that Elijah was under? Would you be willing to take that kind of stand? Let's be honest; it would be really difficult, but Elijah was a bold leader. Maybe he remembered the words of the former Godly leader of Israel, Joshua: "Have I not commanded you? Be strong and courageous. Do not be afraid; do not be discouraged, for the Lord your God will be with you wherever you go" (Joshua 1:9). Elijah was indeed committed in dependence on God.

Of course, what happened next is predictable. The prophets of Baal went first. They prayed to their god, but nothing happened. Matter of fact, they prayed for hours with no results. Finally, something happened, but it's not what you might think. It's actually pretty humorous. Elijah began to taunt and mock them. "Maybe he is sleeping," Elijah proclaimed! "Maybe he's busy or traveling," Elijah exclaimed! "Maybe he went to Buffalo Wild Wings for dinner," Elijah scoffed...okay, I added that one. You get the idea though. Nothing happened because Baal wasn't real. He wasn't God!

Now it was Elijah's turn, and let's be honest, it was really God's turn to show his power and glory. Elijah rebuilt the altar of the Lord that had been cast aside in those days as the people had been worshiping Baal. Then, he ordered the men standing nearby to pour four large jars of water all over the bull offering and the wood. In fact, he ordered them to do it three different times, equaling twelve jars of water. Have you ever tried to burn drenched wood? During the summer, my family and I like to go Up North here in Michigan with our kids for a few days. Most evenings, we gather around the campfire and eat s'mores and enjoy one another's company. One thing is for sure: if it's been raining that day, we don't have an evening campfire. Why? Because water-logged wood does not burn.

This was a profound moment. God was going to show the whole world that he is the one true God through Elijah's passionate boldness. Through Elijah's steadfast faith, God was going to show those false prophets that he has control over his own creation. Even wood that scientifically can't burn when wet will burn when God supernaturally causes it to burn. With everyone's attention glued to Elijah, this was his moment to be God's instrument of repentance. Make no mistake, God receives the glory for what God does, but we can't help but recognize Elijah's commitment, boldness, and character. Some might even argue that this was the greatest spiritual moment of Elijah's life. Notice how the story unfolds in 1 Kings 18:36-39:

> "At the time of sacrifice, the prophet Elijah stepped forward and prayed: 'Lord, the God of Abraham, Isaac and Israel, let it be known today that you are God in Israel and that I am your servant and have done all these things at your command. Answer me, Lord, answer me, so these people will know that you, Lord, are God, and that you are turning their hearts back again.' Then the fire of the Lord fell and burned up the sacrifice, the wood, the stones and the soil, and also licked up the water in the trench. When all the people saw this, they fell prostrate and cried, 'The Lord – he is God! The Lord – he is God!'"

Not only did God send down fire from heaven, but he also caused the fire to "lick up" every drop of water, unquestionably demonstrating his power over all. What happened next? The people repented. The idea of repentance is a change of direction because of a change of attitude. To put it simply, they changed their view of God, and this change led to good actions. This was a dramatic moment. Hundreds, maybe thousands, of people turned from Baal to the one true God. God had dramatically used Elijah to bring a nation back to himself. It was the highlight of Elijah's life up to this point. What a moment!

It's not hard to imagine the exhilaration and gratitude that Elijah was feeling in that moment. I know in my own life how I've felt when God has used me in some powerful way to see someone come to him in salvation. Nothing compares to it. I honestly feel bad for Christians who live for themselves. They have no idea of what they're missing!

The Bible reminds me that I am God's masterpiece prepared by him before the foundations of the world to serve him (Ephesians 2:10), and so are you if Christ is your Savior! It's incredible to think that people were face down on the ground worshiping God because Elijah was willing to be an instrument in God's hands. Make no mistake: God gets the full glory, but don't misunderstand, he uses us to bring himself glory! How incredible is that reality? Wow!

Although what happened next is inconceivable, it is quite common. Victory experiences pushback. We need to realize that success achieved does not eliminate pressure. In fact, it intensifies it. What does this even mean? It means that success is never exhaustive. There is always another challenge to face. There is always another "game to win." There is always more opposition coming your way. Think about it this way. You just "closed the deal" for your company. This is a big moment. You've secured new income and new relationships. It's a partnership that you have dreamed of since you took the job. You spent countless hours developing a strategy, creating a plan, brainstorming ideas, meeting for discussion, and finally convincing your proposed client to partner with you. When that moment happens, it's exhilarating. It feels like the perfect conclusion, until it isn't. Does that "victory" guarantee you that a competing company won't attempt to woo your "grand prize" away from you? Of course not. You can expect that your competition will simply become more aggressive in their approach to defeat you.

Another example of this can be found in college football recruiting. A head coach along with his staff can work tirelessly to secure a verbal commitment from the top-ranked quarterback in the country. This is a big moment for this coach and his staff. He spent countless hours on the phone and through social media with his prized recruit. He even ate dinner with the recruit's parents explaining how he plans to take good care of their son through solid academics, safe social opportunities, and guaranteed care in other areas. The coach leaves the home excited because his work has produced fruit. The young man verbally commits to play football for the coach. The young man's parents are convinced that it's the right thing to do—that is, until Coach Saban from Alabama shows up on their doorsteps. What I am trying to say is that college football recruiting is a cutthroat profession. I have watched several athletes over the years "flip" from one school to another. Nothing is guaranteed until the young man signs his national letter of intent to play football at a particular school, and even then, nothing is certain. The point is that even after a coach secures a great recruit, the "battle" for that recruit is not over. Victory simply brings more challenges. Let's be honest—we want victory, but are we ready for the challenges that come after the victory? It is a completely different reality that most people underestimate.

Past victories don't eliminate future challenges. Elijah's "victory" guaranteed that a greater challenge was coming! The reality is that there is no such thing as "down time" when it comes to challenges. This is why you absolutely must rest after a "victory." You won't have enough stamina or strength for the next challenge immediately. We get a glimpse of this reality in 1 Kings 19:1-5:

> "Now Ahab told Jezebel everything Elijah had done and how he had killed all the prophets with the sword. So Jezebel sent a messenger to Elijah to say, 'May the gods deal with me, be it ever so severely, if by this time tomorrow I do not make your life like that of one of

them.' Elijah was afraid and ran for his life. When he came to Beersheba in Judah, he left his servant there, while he himself went a day's journey into the wilderness. He came to a broom bush, sat down under it and prayed that he might die. 'I have had enough, Lord,' he said. 'Take my life; I am no better than my ancestors.' Then he lay down under the bush and fell asleep. All at once an angel touched him and said, 'Get up and eat.'"

Clearly, when Elijah was used by God to expose the prophets of Baal, Jezebel wasn't present. At this point, however, she found out what had happened, and she's the next challenge for Elijah. He wasn't ready for it. Would he have been ready if it had happened before the famous duel with the prophets of Baal? Probably, but it came after. The last thing Elijah needed was to engage in an immediate challenge right after his victory. The Bible is clear that he needed rest. He was emotionally, physically, mentally, and even spiritually drained.

When you engage with the next challenge instead of getting rest, you run the risk of becoming irrational. To reset the story, Elijah had just slaughtered the 450 prophets of Baal. The evil queen would now surrender (Elijah thought) - except she became only more obstinate. Her "yes men" who perpetuated her corrupt "power thirst" were gone. Now, she was even more outraged than before. Elijah should have gone out of town, to get away, turning off all social media, and putting his iPhone away, but he didn't. He got word that Jezebel was going to come after him, and this news terrified him. He became irrational. How do I know that? Well, because he had just taken on 450 prophets of Baal and the powerful king by himself. He fearlessly stood for truth, and God blessed him. Now, he was terrified of the queen. God had clearly demonstrated that he had much for Elijah to do for his honor and glory. Elijah didn't see it. He was worn out. He was burned out. He needed rest, but he wasn't getting it. His irrational state of mind got worse. He began to wish that he were dead, seeing his life as a failure. How is this possible? It's not only possible; it's probable when you're not resting.

I often use the illustration of "the box" to make my point. It's like having a box over your head, and all you can see is what's in the box. The contents of the box are filled with disappointments, struggles, trials, and temptations. You are limited when you focus on the box. Why? Because there is an entire unseen world outside the box. That's the will of God. God is moving and working even when it's unseen—especially when it's unseen. Even when you can't "feel" God, he is there! Being "boxed in" is not uncommon when we're emotionally spent. We see the worst possible scenario as an absolute for our lives. This is where Elijah was. Just the day before, God had used him in a dramatic and supernatural way. Now, he wanted to die. Now, he thought his life was worthless and powerless. His response was that he "had enough" which is exactly why he needed to rest. We all have a breaking point. We all have a point of no return. We all need a break and a Kit Kat bar. Knowing that point is paramount to our long-term success.

Some of the most discouraging times in life are when we think the pressure is off for a bit, only to realize that it's about to get greater. You just finished—I mean, helped your kid finish his science fair project. Then, he comes to you the very next day asking for help with his history project. You want to bang your head against a wall. What do you do? You start all over again with little to no time in between for rest. It seems endless, doesn't it? One thing I've realized over the years is that I can't be "all things to all people at all times." This even applies to my family. **Don't underestimate the effects of expended energy.** Elijah found himself in the depths of discouragement and fatigue. Why? Because of the energy he had just expended for God. As we take a look back, notice what Elijah's service required of him: *challenging corrupt authority (boldness), persuading the people (emotion & will), performing miracle in God's power (adrenaline & possible anxiety), killing prophets (courage), and running to Jezreel (physical stamina).* Elijah's task was no small challenge. Don't underestimate what facing your everyday and even unique challenges is going to require of you.

The best way to keep from underestimating "rest stealers" is found in a common yet creative battle. We all face this battle, and it morphs into many challenging forms. I'm talking about the "battle of the mind." Over the years, I've watched strong and confident people reduced to great discouragement because they didn't win the battle of the mind. I liken this issue to scratching a mosquito bite. In the moment, it's very satisfying to scratch the infected area, but we all know what comes next: greater pain. It makes it worse. In the same way, we often allow our emotions to lead us because in the moment doing so feels good. There's a certain adrenaline rush, even a gratification. The problem is that the pain that comes next—and it *will* come next—doesn't solve anything. It makes it worse.

Elijah in the moment was "unable" to see the supernatural success of the past. Instead, his focus was on a much lesser threat than what he had just encountered. You might wonder how this could happen. Well, you don't have to look far; it happens to all of us. We begin to be filled with fear, and fear creates an invisible wall blocking truth from leading us. Sometimes it's a predisposition or a certain situation that we struggle with as Timothy did. Timothy was a young pastor feeling the pressure to lead well. The Apostle Paul, as a mentor to young Timothy, challenged him in 2 Timothy 1:7: "For God did not give us a spirit of timidity, but a spirit of power, of love, and of self-discipline." He reminded Timothy that timidity or fear will be overcome in God's power, sacrificial love, and a disciplined mind. We must be led by facts, not by feelings. Feelings will deceive. Facts (or God's truth) will disciple. It's amazing how quickly we forget the facts when we're faced with an immediate challenge. One of the greatest defenses against the deceitfulness of feelings is a strong memory. Remind yourself of what God has already done in your life. Remind yourself of the battles that have already been won in his strength. I would recommend that you journal "spiritual victories" in your life so that you can go back and read about them in your most challenging moments. These memorials can be a huge source of encouragement when you're "not feeling it." Isn't that what God's Word does? It reminds us of God's faithfulness, holiness, and eternal perspective.

After experiencing success, take time to rest. If you try to engage in your own strength, you'll have the same reaction as Elijah. Remember his words: "I have had enough...take my life; I am no better than my ancestors" (1 Kings 19:4b). Elijah felt worthless, powerless, and no more impactful than those before him in removing idol worship from the nation of Israel. That's where feelings can be a big problem. The fact was that Elijah was indeed very different from those ancestors before him. This is why resting after a victory is so important. Interestingly enough, I am writing this section of the book while on vacation. This vacation follows God's using our church and my life in many incredible ways. Our church in recent months during the COVID-19 pandemic was able to receive, assemble, and give out almost 2,000 units of food to our community as a "hub" location through the Genesee County Sheriff's Department. We were also one of the first churches in Genesee County to gather again for worship, encouraging so many. I was able to teach other pastors and encourage their re-gathering process. We also were able to see our online audience grow exponentially. We now have people watching our Sunday gatherings from as far as California and even Africa. God receives all the glory. My point in explaining all of this is that I have recently begun to allow my feelings to override the facts. Fear began to flood my mind, posing the following questions: *"What if certain families don't come back to church?" "What if we don't have enough income to have future ministries?" "What if COVID-19 strikes again in the fall, and we have to start the process all over again?" "What if marriages begin to fall apart?"* It became easy for me to forget about the miracles that God did through the last few months while I was focusing on the "what ifs." This state of mind is unhealthy. This state of mind is dangerous. This state of mind can be a very common problem. This state of mind is overcome by spiritual rest.

Instead of resting, we run to our "Jezreel" right away. The story within the story was that Israel was under a famine curse from God. There had been no rain for more than three years, and now God was going to graciously send rain to water their crops and provide for their animals. The source of the much-awaited storm was going to come from the sea near the town of Jezreel. Instead of going on "vacation," Elijah supernaturally ran ahead of King Ahab's chariot to Jezreel. Why? What was the point? Maybe it was to give the wicked king one last chance to turn from his sin before reaching Queen Jezebel. Maybe it was to ensure that the correct story of what happened at Mount Carmel was told in Jezreel. Maybe it was to see the miracle for himself. Whatever the reason, he should have immediately rested.

What is your "Jezreel?" This is the place of powerful fear, unexpected push-back, and irrational forgetfulness. Elijah made himself vulnerable by "moving forward" when he should have taken a break. Sometimes we look at people who rest as being weak. We allow ourselves to be deceived into thinking that we could handle the pressure that they're "avoiding!" Maybe you've been there looking at a fellow mother, neighbor, church member, or coworker as being weaker than you. You believe in "pushing through!" You think that people who don't "push through" are lazy and weak. The crazy thing is that we judge people's work ethics when we have no idea what their situations truly are. We judge what we see. We see a mother in a mall play-place sitting quietly on a bench while her kids uncontrollably run around. We think to ourselves that if she were a good mother she would be engaging with her kids. We judge her to be inattentive. That's what we see. What we don't see is that she was up half the night tending to her sick husband. We see a church family decide not to participate in this year's outreach event. We think to ourselves that if they were truly dedicated they would be at the annual Trunk-or-Treat ready to serve the community dressed like Spider-Man or The Incredibles or at least the youth pastor. That's what we see. What we don't see is that this family has been up at the church so much that it's starting to create resentment. They need a break just like the mother. We judge what we see. That's dangerous. Why? Because it creates not only a self-righteous attitude toward others but also a false sense of reality for ourselves. You have limitations. The quicker you realize that the better. I applaud the exhausted mother in the mall and the worn-out church family. They're wise; are you? Know your limitations. How can you do that? It's found in response or reaction.

There is a big difference in healthy dialogue and action versus toxic dialogue and action. It's found in what R-word you live by. Elijah RESPONDED in faith at the Mount Carmel duel; he REACTED in fear by running 120 miles south to Beersheba when he was threatened by Queen Jezebel. There's an obvious difference between these two words and what they encompass. When you RESPOND to something, you are in control of your emotions. You are thoughtful and deliberate. You have a "game plan" in how to deal with it. You see the challenge as something that will ultimately benefit your life. You don't allow your circumstances to control you; you control your circumstances the best you can. **Response is grounded in faith.** On the other hand, when you REACT to something, you are not in control of your emotions. You tend to be near-sighted, seeing only impossible challenges in front of you, which causes you to forget past victories. You are thoughtless and spontaneous. You have no idea how to deal with the immediate challenge. You see the challenge as a disaster that is going to harm you. You tend to say things and do things that you'll later regret. **Reaction is grounded in fear.**

You will be ready to respond to the next challenge only when you've refueled yourself in God's truth plus physical and emotional rest. What I have found in my own life is that God's Word is very relevant for my everyday challenges —that is, when I'm actually reading it. What Elijah needed was time alone with God for rejuvenation with no relational "drains" in that moment. He wasn't going to all of a sudden stop being the prophet of God. Just like you're not going to stop being a pastor, accountant, line worker, business owner, father, mother, coach, teacher, etc. You get the idea. Elijah had "big moments" to come, just like you and I do. The lesson in all of this is that we must be ready for those next moments, and we won't be when we're completely worn out. When you're worn out, you help no one, including you.

So, what I've found is that our lives are usually a combination of both response and reaction. In one moment, Elijah was celebrating the greatest spiritual victory Israel had seen in years. In the next moment, Elijah was ready to give up. He was even ready to die. Maybe you're feeling a little like Elijah. Maybe you're feeling like giving up right now. In those difficult moments, you must remind yourself: **What you think and feel in the moment doesn't tell the full story of what's happening.**

If there's ever a time when you need to rest, it's after a "big victory" because challenges are sure to keep coming. We tend to see it the opposite way. We see a greater opportunity. We sense an important moment. We even fear a "closing window of opportunity" if we don't keep striving and pushing forward. Stop underestimating "success fatigue." It's the underrated enemy of success. You have limits. There's a reason that Gatorade is such a successful product in the sports world. When you expend energy, you must replenish energy. When you are mentally stretched, you must mentally rest. When you are physically stretched, you must physically recharge. Healing and rest are often synonymous with one another. It is especially important that you rest after victory and success. Take time to get away from people and get with God in prayer, Bible study, and meditation. Your future impact depends on it.

CHAPTER 8
IMITATIONS ARE EXPOSED

HAVE you ever been duped by an imitation? The other day my wife and I got into a debate with our kids over bottled water, of all things. Our kids were emphatically united (which is ironic because they're never united over anything) that purified bottled water is better than bottled spring water. The funny part about this is that my wife and I believe that it's all the same, and it all probably comes from a tap anyway. Our kids say otherwise. They are convinced that they're right. So, we decided to do a little taste test. They were pretty confident until we exposed the reality that they couldn't tell one from the other. Then, the excuses came. It was so great. Mark up a victory for the parents! We are sure to never let them live this one down. It will probably be brought up at their graduation open house. Of course, there are examples that are much more obvious. If you've ever had a Pepsi or a Coke compared with an off-brand cola, you can probably tell the difference. If you've ever had a pizza from Little Caesars compared with a frozen pizza, you can probably tell the difference. Why? Because the real thing is emphatically better. In a much more dramatic way, do you remember when Rosie Ruiz won the Boston Marathon back in 1980? It was an incredible finish until it was proved that Ruiz cheated and ran only a portion of the race. That was a shocker. She had many people fooled—until she didn't.

No one likes an imitation. Like never before, people are looking for authenticity. There are so many untruths out there in our culture. When you turn on the news channel, you're never truly sure what is real and what is fake. People have lost faith in their pursuit of what is authentic. I honestly believe that the next generation is not going to tolerate imitation. They want what looks, tastes, feels, and is real. They would rather you disagree with them than lie to them. Doesn't it make you well up in frustration and even anger when someone is dishonest with you? We get angry with others, but what about when we're the source of the inauthentic behavior? What about when we're the source of what is not accurate or is even dishonest?

Token rest doesn't fool anyone, including your own body. Rest is not a five-minute break at work in the break room. Rest is not a token day off that's still filled with phone calls, emails, and work projects. Rest is not a quick fix. Rest is deliberate. Rest is concentrated. Rest makes sacrifices. It realizes that you can't be all things to all people at all times. Rest turns off your cellphone. Rest realizes that the supposed emergency can actually wait until Monday. Rest focuses on spiritual, emotional, mental, and physical revitalization. **Rest is not a checkmark on your "to do list."** In other words, you must focus on true rest in the same way that you focus on your career goals. Why? Because you want to be at your absolute best when you're attempting to achieve God's will for your life.

Remember our most recent character Elijah? He had

achieved great victory in God's strength in overcoming the prophets of Baal, but then he became overwhelmed when he didn't receive the rest he so desperately needed. He became irrational and discouraged. What happened next is easy to miss, but it's incredibly important in creating longevity or what I like to call "staying power." Notice the next part of Elijah's education in "Rest 201" in 1 Kings 19:5-9a:

> "Then he lay down under the tree and fell asleep. All at once an angel touched him and said, 'Get up and eat.' He looked around, and there by his head was a cake of bread baked over hot coals, and a jar of water. He ate and drank and then lay down again. The angel of the Lord came back a second time and touched him and said, 'Get up and eat, for the journey is too much for you.' So he got up and ate and drank. Strengthened by that food, he traveled forty days and forty nights until he reached Horeb, the mountain of God. There he went into a cave and spent the night."

Let me paraphrase the above verses. An angel appeared to Elijah and offered him baked bread and a jar of water. He ate and drank and fell back to sleep. Then, the angel woke him again and challenged him to eat and drink some more so that he could effectively travel the 250 miles from Beersheba to Horeb which was Mount Sinai, the mountain of God.

What you need to notice is that the initial "rest" wasn't enough for Elijah. He needed more sleep. What you also need to notice is that the initial "sustenance" provided to him wasn't enough. He needed more bread and water. The angel supernaturally knew what he needed, and he provided for those needs on different occasions. There's probably no better example of someone needing to "crash" than this story of Elijah in the Bible. In application, it should remind us that sometimes we need more than our weekly Sabbath. Sometimes you need extended rest because of your extended efforts. Part of that rest should involve scheduled vacations. Just remember the purpose of vacation. It's to recharge. Also, be warned that if you need a vacation from the vacation when you get back, you'll be just as frustrated and exhausted as you were before you actually went. Don't make this common and frustrating mistake.

"Crash mode" happens to passionate people. It's nothing to be ashamed of when you experience it. Matter of fact, it normally means that you've achieved something worthwhile in your life. It has consumed you for a specific period of time. You've given your blood, sweat, and tears to this project. You have nothing left. You must reset yourself or else you'll pay a steep price. Just like Elijah, each one of us needs a certain amount of rest and sustenance for strength and nourishment. If you take shortcuts now, you will pay the price later. God offers to you what you need to fulfill your purpose. **Your journey to influence demands commitment to a healthy mind and body.** Do yourself and others a favor, and get some extended rest now so that you can be effective later.

Sometimes you can't get everything done that you want done in the timeframe that you desire. In anticipation of my oldest child's graduation open house, my wife gave me a "honey-do" list. Since we had committed to having his open house at our personal residence, there was work to be done. In fact, there was a *lot* of work to be done. The largest out of many projects involved our front lawn landscaping. We decided to remove three over-grown bushes and to put down three yards of stone. Wow! That was challenging! With some much needed help from my friend Marty, we pulled those bushes and their roots out of the ground. That was very difficult and challenging, yet it was not the hardest part. My daughter Victoria and I shoveled all of those thousands of stones and dumped them into the predetermined areas. That was even more difficult, yet it was not the hardest part. The hardest part involved my attempting to shovel out a new path where the lining and edging would go on the far end of the landscaping. Why was that so hard, you might ask? It's because that area in front of my house was filled with rocks barely under the surface of grass and dirt. In other words, every time I stepped on my shovel, I hit a rock and barely went down an inch or more. Needless to say, I became quite frustrated.

To put this experience into context, I had worked hard all day. We began early on a Saturday morning. It was over 90 degrees that day, and I was drenched in sweat thirty minutes into the job. During the course of the day, I changed my shirt multiple times, drank multiple gallons of water, and moved multiple wheelbarrows of stone for hours. My skin was sunburned. My body was tired. My muscles were aching. My strength was gone. What you need to realize though is that with the help of my family, we achieved a lot that day. Over 75% of the area was now beautifully landscaped with stone. I was proud of what we had achieved. Then, I almost made a huge mistake.

That last part of the job was the area that was filled with stones barely under the surface of the ground. I still had to dig out that part of the path, reshaping the area. I decided that I was going to "press on" and finish the job. That was a mistake. I had no energy left. I wanted so desperately to be done, to be finished. This is but a microcosm of a bigger issue that we have as human beings. We are impatient. Instead of embracing the process, we attempt to force production. Because I wanted to be done, I was going to do everything in my power to get the job done that day. It wasn't happening.

As I took my shovel and attempted to dig out the area, I hit stones every time. I started getting frustrated. That frustration turned into panic. My panic almost became tears and anger directed at my family. How could I get to such a place? I needed true rest, not token rest. You see, I told myself that I could do it. I rationalized in my mind that I had taken breaks, had drunk plenty of water, had eaten lunch, and was now ready to complete the job. Maybe you can argue that those moments were more than "token rest," and you might be right. The only thing that I do know for sure is that they were not enough. I had to stop. I'll never forget that moment. I looked at my wife with disappointment and embarrassment in my eyes and told her that I couldn't finish the job right then. I'll never forget her response. She looked at me with affirming eyes and told me that it was going to be okay. I needed to hear that. I needed to know that it was okay to be weak. I needed to know that it was okay to be tired. I needed to know that it was okay to take a much needed and much deserved break from my labor. Let me tell you that it's okay for you to be tired. Maybe you've not heard it enough, but you need to know that it's okay to be "spent." I'm not God. You're not God. We are all finite beings, meaning that we have limitations. It's really important that we are not only hearing it for ourselves, but we are also telling the people in our lives the same thing. When you expect your husband or wife or children to be superhuman, you are setting them up for failure. Be gracious enough to encourage people in their frailty. You'll need the same grace at some point.

I walked away from the front yard that Saturday early evening ending my plan to complete the job. After putting the tools away, I took a shower. After I took a shower, I laid on the couch and rested. The next day was Sunday, so I didn't pick up my shovel at all. Instead, I preached, led, and encouraged our church family. The rest of the afternoon I rested some more. I laid on the couch and watched Netflix with my wife. I went for a walk in the early evening. Just like Elijah, I needed more rest for the challenge ahead. Elijah ate, drank, and then slept. That was round one. Then, he repeated the same process. Why? Because he needed more than what he thought he needed at first. I was no different.

On Monday morning everything was different. I was mentally recharged. My muscles were healed and no longer stiff and sore. Most importantly, my psyche was healthy. I had gotten the rest that I needed. When I attacked the rock-filled area, this time it was different. I was working at full capacity of mind, body, and even soul. I took the shovel and even an ax and promptly created a path for the weed liner and edging. Was it challenging? Sure. Was it discouraging? Nope. I was ready for this challenge. By lunch time, the job was completed. A brand new landscape in the front of our house with new edging and beautiful stones looked amazing. In fact, our neighbors are still complimenting us on the new look.

What's the lesson? Well, there's actually a few lessons to learn. The first lesson is that we all have limitations. That means you too. I don't care how big and strong you are. I don't care how smart and talented you are. I don't care how gregarious your personality is. Everyone, and I mean everyone, has limitations. Know your limitations. When you attempt to "push through" fatigue and exhaustion, it will only produce discouragement, moodiness, and ultimately more pain. The second lesson is that it's okay to complete the "project" at a later time. It was so hard for me to walk away from the project that Saturday night without it being done. I felt like a failure. I felt weak. The truth is that I wasn't a failure, but I was weak. That's okay. It's normal. I had expended all of my energy that day, and there was nothing left to give. We all come to these "crash mode" points. When that happens, it's time for rest. The third lesson is that you can't "cheat" rest. Your body is not falling for it. Even though I had experienced small doses of rest during the day, those small doses weren't enough to sustain me any longer. It was time for extended, not token, rest. We've all been there, but unfortunately we tend to make excuses and "cheat rest."

Isolate, expose, and eliminate your greatest threats to rest. Have you ever made an excuse for not doing something that you're supposed to be doing? Of course you have. From procrastination to overeating to laziness to fear, we're all guilty. Realize this: It's always easier to remain in your present condition of dysfunction. I'm challenging you to be different! I'm challenging you to take responsibility in an area of your life that is important to your future. I'm asking you to be honest with yourself as you look into the spiritual mirror of your life. The fact is that when we look into a mirror there are certain things that are undeniable. We can't cheat a mirror; it emphatically exposes the absolute truth about our present appearance.

Even so, we live in a generation of denial. A hilarious example of this is what my girls found in cyberspace the other day. My family is crazy about taking pictures. I mean, off the charts crazy. We can hardly go a day without my wife or girls wanting to take pictures. The funny part about this is that guys don't care. Take the picture, and be done. We don't care if we had a hair out of place or if the angle of the camera made us look fat. We just don't care. "Please take the picture before our heads explode" is our attitude. On the other hand, my girls recently found an app that changes your appearance. It can make you look tanner, thinner, taller, and somehow happier. It's ridiculous in a funny way. Why? Because it's not authentic—it's imitation. I told my girls that I don't want them using that app on me. Do you know why? Because it will give me a false sense of security that isn't accurate. Accuracy is a funny thing. It exposes. Sometimes we need to be exposed. Sometimes we can't deny the blemishes, which means that we need to do something about them. Maybe that time for you is right now.

There are three major reasons that we "cheat rest." Because they are not profound, you might already recognize one of them in your life. It is time to respond to them. The first one is being **fear consumed**. We live in a perpetual state of fear, always thinking about the "worst case scenario" which doesn't allow for rest. I counsel people all the time who are going through difficult circumstances. Part of their struggle is their imagination. They struggle to see their challenge in the moment. Instead, they see their present challenge splintering into multiple other challenges. In other words, they create overwhelming scenarios that are not impossible but very unlikely. See if you can relate to this scenario: *"I'm going to be late to work. I heard yesterday that Jeff was late to work, and he got fired. That's not good. It's already true that my boss doesn't really care for me, because he rarely comes by my cubicle to talk to me. I must be in* *danger of losing my job. I saw him laughing the other day talking about sports with James. I'm definitely in danger of losing my job, and now it's going to happen for sure because I'm going to be late. That's surely what cost Jeff his job!"*

Have you ever found yourself spiraling out of control in your mind? The above scenario is an example of a "rest robber." Instead of focusing on facts, we jump to ridiculous conclusions. One fact that I didn't consider was that Jeff was making disparaging comments about the company on social media after being reprimanded for sexual misconduct. Another fact that I didn't consider is that James is my boss's cousin. They actually played high school sports together. Can you see how it is so easy to jump to conclusions and fear the worst possible scenario? We do it all the time.

Fear can be a paralyzing thing! It can steal your rest even though you're resting. Remember what we talked about in an earlier chapter: You need the spiritual balance of physical, emotional, mental, and spiritual rest. Often, our minds are the enemy's greatest target. One statement I've made over and over in counseling is that "the battle is in the mind!" If you don't win the battle in the mind, you won't win the battle in your hands or feet either.

Sometimes our fear is generated from pride. We fear failure so much that we work extra hard to ensure that we don't fail. This kind of fear often comes from the sin of comparison. We're afraid that someone we know could be more successful or popular than we are. As a result, we work harder than usual to keep this from happening. Let's be honest, our motivations are totally "off" in this kind of fear. We care more about what people think than we care about our own health. Fear is debilitating!

Another reason why we "cheat rest" is because we get

consumed with a **"window of opportunity."** When an opportunity comes along, we think to ourselves that there is no time for rest. This is the opportunity we've always waited for, and now is the time to seize it! We think that if we don't "push ourselves" *right now*, we'll never get this opportunity again. We've already discussed in a previous chapter the fallacies of "pushing through" when you need rest. On rare occasions we do need to push through when there's little gas in the tank. The problem is that we've made this the norm instead of the exception. Let me help you with a sobering reality that I'm still trying to learn in my late-40s. There will always be another contract to get signed at work. There will always be another person to counsel in ministry. There will always be another class to take. There will always be another burden to carry. Do you understand the point? Being able to discern when to engage and when to "bow out" is tremendously important to having balance in your life. It will come only when you commit to having boundaries.

I love to watch the TV show *Shark Tank*. I always find it fascinating to hear the pitches of young entrepreneurs who are looking to "jump start" their careers with their unique inventions. They come in and share the reasons their products are worth investing in and how they will change the world. Of course, their objective is to convince Mark Cuban and the other wealthy business owners to front them the cash so that their project can get off the ground. In exchange for the money, the "shark" receives a certain percentage of the future company's earnings. It can be a good deal for both parties, but if the "sharks" don't think the young entrepreneur's plan is going to benefit them, they're out. Why is that? It's because they've learned to be shrewd with their money. In other words, they know that you can't invest in every supposed novel idea that comes along. In the end, that would be irresponsible and unhealthy for their business model. They are very careful what they invest in, and that's one of the major reasons why they are so successful.

Instead of seeing what you're going to miss by not investing in the current window of opportunity, see what you're going to gain by saying "no" right now! There was a man in our church who was pushing hard for a promotion at his job not long ago. He worked hard to get the promotion that he so desperately wanted, but it didn't turn out to be as great as he had anticipated. What he learned quickly was that this promotion was going to bring a lot of new stresses into his life through a whole new set of challenges. He got to the place where he almost had an emotional breakdown. I can relate. I've been there. I wonder if my friend would go back and change things if he had the opportunity to do so. Was it worth it? You need to ask yourself the same question. Is it worth it? Sometimes our biggest enemy is impatience! God is not playing some twisted game up in heaven where he wants you to practically kill yourself to succeed. That is completely contrary to his plan for your life. The fact is that the "window of opportunity" issue connects back to the previous thief of fear. We scare ourselves into thinking, "What if I miss this opportunity and never get another one as a result?" This kind of mentality limits the power of God in your life. Obviously, the previous sentence is impossible since God cannot be limited. So, maybe, we need to start seeing God for who He truly is. All opportunities come from him. Trust him, and find balance.

The biggest reason why I believe we "cheat rest" is what I like to call the **"Superman complex."** "I don't need the rest" becomes our prideful reaction out of disillusionment. We view rest as a detriment to our day. We view rest as something the "weak" need. We view rest as something we can negotiate. When I was a youth pastor, there were two absolutes that drove my youth ministry. They were pizza and Cedar Point. Okay, I'm kidding, kind of. What I'm saying is that both were big "hits" with the kids. Every summer (besides summer camp), the highlight for the kids was taking a trip to Cedar Point. At almost every activity, there was pizza. Who doesn't love pizza? Well, for one, my wife who actually hid pizza from me the other day, but that's a story for another time. Anyway, let's describe the actual days that we'd take our youth group to Cedar Point.

It began really early. Basically, I was awake and in the shower at 5:00 AM. Then, I would head to the church and make sure the buses were ready to go. From getting permission forms signed to telling kids the rules, it was always a madhouse. Then, we'd board the buses and drive to Sandusky, Ohio. That was at least a three-hour drive, but often it became even longer because the buses had governors which regulated their speed to a maximum of 55 MPH. We'd stop for a bathroom and snack break normally in Monroe, Michigan, at which time I'd have to keep track of each student while prodding them to hurry along. Then, we'd arrive at the park at about 10 or 11 AM. We'd get the tickets to the kids and let them go until mid-afternoon at which point we'd have a check-in with all the middle schoolers at the Ferris wheel. The goal was to make sure they were all still alive and staying out of trouble.

Cedar Point day was always long, hot, and tiring. Going from ride to ride, you were always on the run. Why? Because you wanted to maximize the day. "Let's get as much out of the day as possible" was the mantra. For about twelve hours, we'd all race from ride to ride, often standing in the blazing sun waiting to board the *Power Tower, Top-Thrill Dragster, Millennium Force,* and many other exhilarating rides. From the lack of sleep to the hot weather to the emotional excitement to the miles of walking, by the end of the day, you were completely exhausted. Then, the true challenges would begin.

If you've ever taken a group to Cedar Point, you're about to feel the hairs on the back of your neck stand up with what I'm about to say. You know the drill. You give your group the famous "meet back at the bus" time. You threaten their lives if they're not back on time. Why? Because you have no control. You can't stick with every kid, so you are forced to trust their responsible hearts. I know, many of you are hilariously laughing right now. Why? Because middle schoolers don't have a single mature bone in their bodies, let alone responsible hearts. Therefore, you are at their mercy. Sure, you put them into groups. Maybe you even put them with leaders. But, let's be honest, even the leaders can forget the time, especially if they're young adults. So, 9:00 PM comes, and half the group is back on time. You wait, and you wait. Now it's 9:10 PM, and 2/3 of the group is back. You wait, and you wait. Now it's 9:20 PM, and you're still waiting for Johnny and his "pack of rats" to come back to the bus. You begin to imagine yourself just leaving him in Sandusky, Ohio, and then you realize that his parents would probably call for your resignation. You change your mind, and you wait some more. Eventually, he shows up profusely apologizing when you show him the time. You're so mad, but you just want to go. Finally, everyone is back on the bus. You're off! Home sweet home, here we come! It's 9:35 PM; you're completely exhausted; you have three hours to drive (if you're lucky) before you arrive home.

For many years I didn't prepare for what was next. The hardest part of the entire day was the drive home. Why? Because at this point I had been awake for almost 24 hours by the time the activity was complete. That drive home was treacherous in more ways than one. It began when the bus that had been louder than life on the drive down became silent as a morgue on the way back. Everyone falls asleep including the adult leaders. It's at that moment where I felt completely alone. Looking back on this experience, I find it somewhat humorous and even frightening that everyone trusted me in my current state of mind to get them home safely. It then turns into a battle of the will. Can I stay awake? Will I stay awake? Will we get home safely? I know what you're thinking right now: *"I will never let my kid go to Cedar Point with the church ever again!"* Before you come to that conclusion, it could and would have been different had I established the proper boundaries in my life. More on that later. Back to the ride home. This is where it gets crazy.

I remember on one occasion coming home from Cedar Point where I was really struggling. I was driving our massive 66-passenger bus down the highway, and I was trying my best to stay awake. Looking back on it, I wish someone would have videotaped me. It would be hilarious to watch now, but everyone else was asleep, as I earlier stated. Starting to nod in and out, I began slapping myself in the face. Then, when that wasn't working, I started dumping water on my head and down my shirt. The most memorable moment, though, came when I slammed on the brakes in the middle of the highway. That woke everyone up! Wow—why would I do that? Well, because I was sure someone was walking right in front of my bus. I was so exhausted that I was hallucinating. I couldn't think straight. I couldn't see straight. I was struggling badly. That's what happens when you act as if you're "superman." Thankfully, God in his grace made sure that we all made it home safely.

Before you judge my immaturity, are you guilty of similar experiences? We arrogantly think, "I can handle this!" We proudly think, "I'm strong enough!" We unwisely think, "I'm able!" The fact is that none of us are capable of maximum impact without the balance of spiritual, emotional, and physical rest in our lives. Had I gone to bed earlier than usual the night before the event, I would have been more prepared to handle the strenuousness of the event. Had I delegated more, I could have had someone else who was more rested drive home or at least share the responsibility. Had I taken a break in the middle of the day and rested, even that decision would have better prepared me for the grueling drive home. I did none of those things. Why? Because I am "superman!" Sure, I never said those exact words, but my actions or lack of actions exposed my pride.

Another underrated point in dealing with the "superman complex" is that if you have to do everything yourself, then your structure is a failing structure. In the business world, your company should be able to excel when you're not present. In relationships, your children should be able to excel when you're not present. For example, my middle child is about to start college. She is going to be more than 300 miles away from me. I am trusting that I have taught her well. I am trusting that I have modeled values and absolutes for her to now embrace. I am trusting that she can function independent of me. Often, the "superman complex" is the result of being bad at delegation. If you're trying to do everything yourself, the pain is just beginning. You can't be all things to all people. You might have heard that somewhere already.

Be reminded of this obvious reality: *Imitation is eventually exposed!* Token rest doesn't fool anyone, including your own body. If you take shortcuts now, you will pay the price later. Stop making excuses. Stop "cheating" rest! Elijah learned this lesson the hard way. He needed more than he thought he needed. He needed extended rest. Will you be willing to prioritize true, authentic rest? Start making plans to rest. Do yourself a favor and commit to extended rest now so that you can have an extended impact later. Rest positions you for longevity. Elijah needed rest as the mental battle was just beginning.

CHAPTER 9
FIGHTING DISILLUSIONMENT

ONE OF THE biggest mistakes that we make is prioritizing physical rest without prioritizing mental, emotional, and spiritual rest. We hear in our culture all the time about fitness. Our society is very image conscious. A friend of mine who has committed himself to bodily exercise is always trying to talk me into joining the gym with him. While America actually has an obesity problem, it hasn't slowed down the commercials, pop-up ads on social media, or the multiple professional health coach options out there.

It was no different in the first century. The Apostle Paul leveraged the same cultural priority in his day to remind people of an even greater priority than physical exercise. We previously referenced the next verse, but let's read it again and then dig into its context. 1 Timothy 4:8 says, "For physical training is of some value, but godliness has value for all things, holding promise for both the present life and the life to come." The Apostle Paul is reminding his readers that while physical training is important, spiritual training is even more important. Why did he even need to say this? It was because he was combating a common heresy in that day that actually twisted the physical into an "anything goes" mentality. There was a false belief that was beginning to gain steam that claimed that anything that was physical was inherently evil. Therefore, since everything physical was considered evil, this belief led to gross amounts of debauchery in the forms of drunkenness, sexual immorality, and anything that led to pleasure. The people figured that the physical would eventually be destroyed anyway, so they lived in unquenchable pleasure. In a strange and twisted way, the people unknowingly were actually worshiping the very physical that they had earlier condemned. They were confused and disillusioned.

So, the Apostle Paul fights this disillusionment by teaching young Timothy that the physical actually does matter, a view that rejects the false teachers' views. He does this by showing the connection between the physical and the spiritual, but he doesn't stop there. He reminds Timothy that while the physical is important, the spiritual is the ultimate priority. He challenges Timothy in verse 12 to be influential in the lives of others as follows: "Don't let anyone look down on you because you are young, but set an example for the believers in speech, in conduct, in love, in faith and in purity." Remember, Timothy had a timid disposition. It would have been very easy for him to get disillusioned with the pressure that he was facing as a young pastor. That's why his mentor told him not to let "anyone look down on you." In other words, whatever someone thinks of you doesn't matter. What matters is your integrity! What matters is your purity! What matters is your love! What ultimately matters is your faithfulness to God! Sometimes it's easy to take our eyes off Christ and put them on our abilities or lack of abilities, our experiences or lack of experiences, our knowledge or lack of knowledge. It's in these moments that we forget who our anchor truly is. It's easy then to become disillusioned with life.

This is exactly what happened to Elijah. He was facing false teaching just like Timothy. He was facing outside oppression just like Timothy. He was in a position of leadership just like Timothy. The difference was that he didn't have a life-coach like the Apostle Paul steering him away from the edge of the cliff of spiritual disaster. At this point, his victory over the prophets of Baal was in the distant past. The effects of that victory brought new pressure, causing him to lose all confidence in his purpose. **Past courage doesn't guarantee present confidence.** We've all been there. Every single week I get up to preach feeling this tension. I could have preached a powerful message the week before in which I was faithful to the text, clear to my audience, interesting with illustrations, and do you know what that means for the next week? Absolutely nothing. What I mean is that I have to do it all over again, and that's never easy. Sometimes my study comes easily, but there are weeks when I just don't know how to communicate what I'm studying or even understand it myself, for that matter. That's called being human. Maybe a more relatable illustration was when I was playing baseball as a kid. I could come to the plate and crush a pitch over the centerfielder's head one moment, and then weakly ground out to the pitcher the next. That's the nature of the sport. It's also the nature of our hearts when they're not fully fixed on Christ. I find it to be true that when I focus more on Christ, my preaching is more impactful no matter what the delivery was. Unfortunately, it is so easy to lose sight of this reality.

Elijah lost his focus. He was completely disillusioned with his present conditions. His biggest mistake was that he failed to remember the goodness of God in the recent past.

He was weak, not only physically, but also spiritually. How does this happen to us? I believe it's the result of spiritual laziness. We slowly grow distant from God. Maybe you're feeling this. Maybe it's caused you a lot of recent turmoil in your life. Please realize that there is a cause-and-effect principle in play. James 4:8 tells us, "Come near to God and he will come near to you. Wash your hands, you sinners, and purify your hearts, you double-minded." If you want to sense the presence of God in your life, you must be in the Word of God. You must be in personal prayer. You must have a deliberate and active dependence on God. Victory in the past doesn't guarantee victory in the future unless you keep your focus on Christ.

Elijah was in a bad place. He was completely disillusioned. He was physically exhausted. He was mentally exhausted. He was spiritually exhausted. To reset our story, God had used him greatly to overcome the profound threat of false worship in Israel. The people who had been worshiping false gods were now refocused on the one true God. This was a huge victory! Remember, that after big victories, come big challenges. If you take a bone from a dog, or a bottle from a baby, or shopping from a woman, or sports from a man, you're going to be in for a big-time fight. Elijah had "taken" leadership and influence from a wicked king and queen. They were furious and ready to react. After the evil queen threatened to kill Elijah, he began to spiral away from faith and into fear.

One of the most defining moments of Elijah's disillusionment came after God had sent him to Mount Horeb to worship. When Elijah arrived, he had another encounter with God. What happens next explains his outlook and our often misplaced state of mind. 1 Kings 19:9b-10 says,

"And the word of the Lord came to him: 'What are you doing here, Elijah?' He replied, 'I have been very zealous for the Lord God Almighty. The Israelites have rejected your covenant, torn down your altars, and put your prophets to death with the sword. *I am the only one left*, and now they are trying to kill me too.'"

"No one understands!" "No one cares!" "I'm the only one left!" "I'm all alone!" "What's the point?"—these are the statements of a disillusioned heart. We can get to that dangerous place where we have no hope and begin to believe the lies that surround us. That was Elijah. He was allowing his emotions to lead him. How he felt is what he believed. It's in these moments that we need to be reminded of the actual truth.

It's amazing how quickly we forget. I think kids are a great illustration of this reality. I can't tell you how many times my kids over the years have claimed favoritism. Whether it's a bigger scoop of ice cream or different bed time hours or birthday presents, my kids are watching and looking to accuse. My wife and I have gotten to the point where we buy our kids the same number of Christmas presents no matter what the actual cost of each gift is, so that we can avoid the favoritism debate. One time in the thick of an argument over our supposed love for one of our children over the others, my wife shrewdly and brilliantly looked at our children and told them all, and I quote, (This is a worthy quotation and deserves a place in the parenting hall of fame): *"I don't love one of you more than the others; you all equally annoy me the same!"* I'll never forget that moment. I don't know if I've ever been more proud of my wife. That was a *drop the mic* moment. I laughed so hard. I'm still laughing over that rebuttal.

When I think back to my kids' accusations, I think to myself that their biggest mistake was forgetfulness. They had forgotten the long hours we spent doing science projects. They had forgotten the long trips to soccer games and band competitions. They had forgotten the iPods, iPhones, and X-boxes that we had purchased for them. They had forgotten the pizza dinners, birthday parties, class parties, fun vacations, and everything else under the sun that we had done for them. The fact is that we didn't show favoritism, and they'd realize that if they'd take the time to remember. We've proved our faithfulness to each one of them. We've proved our compassion to each one of them. We've proved our sacrifice to each one of them. The numbers don't lie. The facts can be substantiated. The reality is evident and clear. The problem is that in the moment of a supposed "injustice," all they could see was the present.

Elijah was no different. All he could see was the present. He had forgotten the past. Remember, even before he experienced his huge victory, God had made it clear to him that he wasn't alone. In 1 Kings 18, Elijah had met up with another prophet of God who proceeded to inform Elijah that he had hidden one hundred prophets of God from the evil King Ahab and Queen Jezebel. Elijah knew this. What I'm trying to say is that even when the nation was at its worst, he wasn't alone. Even before the people's hearts were fully turned back to God, he wasn't alone. Those were the facts that he ignored.

It's so easy for us to forget the facts while following our feelings. We begin to feel sorry for ourselves, which steals rest and substitutes anxiety. We have little to no confidence because we have "shortened the glance" into seeing only what's in front of our faces. The result of this is a loss of purpose. We quickly find ourselves drifting in and out of reality. We quickly find ourselves existing instead of thriving. We quickly find ourselves disillusioned in despair. We quickly find ourselves "going through the motions" without any real purpose or plan. This is how low Elijah had come. He was at Mount Horeb, also known as Mount Sinai. He had returned to the sacred place where God had met Moses and given his laws for the nation. This was the place where the Ten Commandments had been given. This was a special place for worship. This is where Elijah was, but he wasn't in a proper state of mind to understand, let alone embrace this reality. That's why God asks him in verse 9: *"What are you doing here?"* Elijah's response proved his disillusionment. All he could see was his present conditions.

Is that all you can presently see? We need to realize that feeling sorry for ourselves and focusing on the negative in our lives will never fix our problems. Sometimes, I look around at children playing outside and think to myself how amazing it would be to be a kid again. Not a care in the world—how great would that be? I could go outside during the summer and play wiffleball with my friends until I was drenched in sweat. Then, I'd go jump in my pool and cool off. After I dried myself off, I'd go inside the house and get myself the biggest ice cream bar without a single calorie concern. That's the life! Wow! I could eat as much as I wanted without gaining a single pound. I could stay up late watching movies and sleep in until I wanted to get up. I could hang out with friends, go out to eat, stay up late, and play every sport that I enjoy. Do you know what the best part of it would be? My parents would pay for it all and make it all happen for me! Here's the thing: that's what being a kid is about, and we all get to enjoy some level of that happiness for a limited period of time in life. Then, adulthood comes. With adulthood comes great challenges. They don't go away either; they just change shape and appearance. The quicker we embrace this reality the better it will be for us. Although life is never going to be easy, it doesn't have to be overwhelming when we trust in God. He has every one of our days measured. He's faithful.

Trust is always interconnected to rest. It's almost always guaranteed that if you're not trusting God, you're not resting. When Elijah became irrational, ignoring what he mentally already knew, he wasn't resting. There is a major reason why he was in this state of mind. It goes back to feeling alone. Have you ever felt alone? We've all been there. **One of the greatest ploys of the enemy is to cause you to feel that you are all alone.** Very few of us like to be alone. From walking into a restaurant to sitting in church to going to a ballgame to flying on a plane—in most situations, we like to be in a community and not just near people, but *with* people. Our family and friendships matter to us. Have you ever wondered why they're so important to us? A lot of it has to do with connection and relatability. We love to connect with people who have the same heritage, hobbies, and values that we do. I personally love to sit at a sporting event with a friend enjoying "our" team winning the game. In an even more impactful sense, I cherish the times that I have had with my family over the years teaching them about God and enjoying their activities. This side of "together" is the positive side that every one of us understands and participates in at some level. We need community. We love community. It brings us comfort. It's necessary for our growth.

Feeling alone is anything but restful. We become anxious. We worry about the "what-ifs." We are quick to internalize our struggles in a way that magnifies a false reality. What I'm trying to say is that when we "feel alone," we tend to have little to no hope that our circumstances can be reversed. The biggest takeaway that I could leave you with right now is that you are truly not alone. You are not alone in the struggle to raise your kids. You are not alone in your struggle to balance your hectic schedule. You are not alone in your job frustrations. You are not alone in suffering loss. You are especially not alone in your struggle to daily love Jesus supremely. I had the opportunity to share some of my struggles with a dear friend not that long ago, and something very profound happened. He looked at me and told me how encouraging that conversation was to him. You might be wondering how my struggles could be an encouragement to him, and the answer is quite simple. Before that conversation, he felt alone. He felt as though he were "the only one." He felt "surrounded on every side." Here's the point: he felt his situation was unique to him. After our conversation, he walked away realizing that he could handle his present circumstances because others just like him have been able to do it. I want to encourage everyone reading this book to be willing to share your struggles with other people. Be humble enough to help. That's right! When you are open and honest about your own issues, it's a huge help to others! Imagine that! The people in your life need to know that you're not perfect. You will be amazed at how your transparent vulnerability will inspire them in their moments of greatest need. No one has it all together. We all have issues and struggles. We all experience unmet expectations. James, the half-brother of Jesus, said it perfectly in James 5:16: "Therefore, confess your sins to each other and pray for each other so that you may be healed. The prayer of a righteous person is powerful and effective." You are not alone!

Sometimes our greatest disillusionments in life come because we're looking for the wrong thing in the moment. Have you ever really expected something or even wanted it, but you didn't get it? You expected God to remove your difficult boss, but instead he put you in position to spend more time with him. You expected God to "fix" your strong-willed child, but instead he began to expose your prideful treatment of that child. You expected God to "solve" your financial problems, but instead he revealed your priority issue of being obsessed with money. What God did is that he gave you the unexpected! You didn't see it coming, and frankly, you wouldn't have wanted it if you had seen it coming. We've all been there. In the moment you were terribly disappointed, but over time it became evident that there was something better for you to experience than what you initially expected and wanted. This is the place where Elijah now finds himself. Notice what God does next. It would be good for us to learn this valuable lesson.

When you're tired and discouraged, you need to rest in who God really is. He is not your genie in the lamp who gives to you whatever self-centered desire that you want. He is not your travel agent who gives you every self-centered experience that you want. What's sadly happened in Christian culture is that we see God in the "big" things. For example, the false church of the Prosperity Gospel has duped thousands of people into believing that God will make them healthy, wealthy, and prosperous if they will follow him. Unfortunately, many people see God as a "spiritual slot machine" looking to make their lives easier. Nothing could be further from the truth. God is not looking to make you rich; God is looking to make you righteous. When you read about this false teaching, you might be thinking: "I absolutely agree with this! I'm behind what you're saying! The 'Prosperity Gospel' is false teaching! We must avoid it!" You would be right, but that's somewhat obvious. What about the not-so-obvious stuff?

There are other "big" ways that we see God falsely too. Even if our doctrine is correct, our practice can be confused. What I mean is that we talk about the "presence of God" as if God shows up only in our emotional worship times with the praise band or in the massive conferences led by well-known speakers or even in the Sunday sermon "tearjerker" illustrations. We limit God's presence to something "big!" It's no wonder that we quite often don't "feel" close to God beyond these moments. We go to church for an experience but don't regularly read our Bibles. It's why we struggle with disillusionment: we are misunderstanding who God really is and what he really does. Our relationship with God is limited; it might even be shallow. We need to be connected to God beyond the "big" moments into the "little" moments. It's the little moments that prepare us for the big moments!

Let's see this fleshed out in Elijah's life. Elijah had just performed the miraculous: Hundreds, even thousands of Israelites had turned their hearts back to God. This was the proverbial highlight of his prophetic career. But, like any moment, the emotion and adrenaline wore off. The pressure mounted once again because, as we previously stated, the enemies of God don't stop attacking. Understand this reality: *If Elijah had maintained a healthy day-to-day dependence on God, this disillusionment that he experienced would not have happened.* **Learn to rest in God on a daily basis.** It was time for God to show Elijah who he really was. Notice 1 Kings 19:11-13:

> "The Lord said, 'Go out and stand on the mountain in the presence of the Lord, for the Lord is about to pass by.' Then a great and powerful wind tore the mountains apart and shattered the rocks before the Lord, but the Lord was not in the wind. After the wind there was an earthquake, but the Lord was not in the earthquake. After the earthquake came a fire, but the Lord was not in the fire. And after the fire came a gentle whisper. When Elijah heard it, he pulled his cloak over his face and went out and stood at the mouth of the cave. Then a voice said to him, 'What are you doing here, Elijah?'"

God's revelation of himself was not what Elijah could have expected. Think about it: Elijah had previously witnessed God bring down fire from the sky to dramatically consume his sacrifice. This was an amazing demonstration of power. While God absolutely demonstrates his power in big ways, he also demonstrates his power in simple ways.

God is in control. Do you believe that? Honestly, I struggle with that statement when I can't see the "end from the beginning!" I know that I am not alone. The fear of the unknown is often a huge thief in our lives. It brings so much anxiety and fear that we often default to panic mode just as Elijah did. The interesting thing is that Elijah mentally grasped the presence of God in the moment. The Bible tells us that after he heard the gentle whisper, he pulled his cloak over his face and went out and stood at the mouth of the cave (vs. 12-13). He knew it was God, yet he wasn't moved emotionally to trust God. Why? Because he still was clouded by his circumstances. The lesson that God was attempting to teach Elijah is profound. We must not miss it as Elijah initially did. It is often the answer to a dependent heart.

God is in control when you cannot see it. God was working in Israel, and he's working all around you too. His plan will come to fruition in our lives. We must realize that he is working "behind the scenes" to bring himself glory through your obedience. God had the ability to move the hearts of his people back to him even if Elijah wasn't seeing it. That is exactly what he was doing. The unspectacular whisper didn't seem like anything special, but it was a symbol of the miraculous process of Godly change. Please be encouraged by this part of the story! As a parent, you might not be seeing the spiritual progress that you would like in your kids' lives. In these moments, remember that God's Word will never return void in their lives. Stay committed. Stay faithful, especially when you're not seeing immediate results. As a spouse, you might be feeling the same discouragement. Pray. Model. Serve. Remember, God is at work even if you aren't seeing the changes that you'd like to see in your spouse. There are a million other relational examples that we could mention. The point is that God is trustworthy; he is working! Elijah needed to realize that even if he couldn't "see it" or "feel it," God was working in the hearts of his people. Unfortunately, we have a hard time perceiving what we cannot immediately see.

On a particular Sunday I was preaching on how to handle the unexpected in our lives. It was Christmastime, and the story of Mary and Joseph was the theme. Mary was a "nobody" from a "nowhere" town when the angel Gabriel informed her of her role in the birth of the Messiah. Joseph was an average guy who thought he was going to marry a woman from Nazareth without any drama. Of course, God placed them into the wonderful narrative of God coming down to redeem mankind. The point of the message was that we need to trust God "one step at a time." I brought a young man named Jake on stage to illustrate this reality. I blindfolded him and twirled him around a few times to the point of him being discombobulated. He didn't have any idea of where he was or where to go next. That is exactly the point. Proverbs 3:5-6 says, "Trust in the Lord with all your heart and lean not on your own understanding; in all your ways submit to him, and he will make your paths straight." We are called to trust God with all of who we are without trying to figure out the next step. Acting as God would, I pointed Jake in the right direction, and I told him to start walking. The illustration was perfect because Jake couldn't see where he was going. All he knew was that he needed to trust what I was telling him. Of course, the temptation to "lean on his own understanding" was there. He could have thought to himself, "What if I walk into the podium?" or "What if I fall off the stage?" Those would have been natural concerns. Obedience has at its foundation, trust. We trust God enough to do what he says. Often, we think of that in terms of what *not* to do. We avoid drunkenness, the love of money, and living for the "here and now" because we trust God. What if it's more than that? What if submitting to God is bigger than that? What if submitting to God is more about what we should be doing than what we should not be doing? You see, God demands that we trust him enough to live for him on a regular basis. What that means is that we accept vulnerability, knowing that God is right there with us.

As Jake reluctantly moved toward the end of the stage, the inevitable was about to take place... Or was it? The crowd was riveted wondering how I was going to keep him from falling off the stage. I could have tried talking him down, which probably would have led to his falling. Let's be honest, that's what everyone thought I was going to do.

That's what he probably thought I was going to do. That is faulty theology. Why? Because God is the one who "makes our paths straight," not us. God is the one who provides for us in our weakness. God is the one who meets us where we are when we need him. Elijah couldn't overcome Jezebel on his own. He just couldn't. All God wanted him to do was to "keep walking down the path." When the time came for God to inject his power into Elijah, he would faithfully do so. Remember, God had done it before. In the illustration, I met Jake at the edge of the stage, and I lifted him off the stage to safety. What an amazing picture of what God did for Elijah at Mount Carmel and what he does for us! We are to trust him, knowing that when the time comes where we cannot succeed on our own, he will be there to "lift us up" in his power. In the meantime, one day at a time; one step at a time; one challenge at a time.

Elijah was looking for the "loud, powerful, and supernatural" just as he had experienced at Mount Carmel, but God often works in the quietness of an obedient heart. To look for God only in something "big" like a church gathering, conference, rally, or from a world-renowned speaker is to put God in a box! You are in danger of completely missing him because he is often found gently whispering in the quietness of a humble heart. Are you listening for God? Step back from the noise and activity of your busy life and listen humbly and quietly for his guidance. It may come when you least expect it.

The only true way to fight disillusionment is through intimacy. **Intimacy is the remedy to noise.** Elijah needed to pray, to worship, and to remember God's goodness. It's not an accident that God took him to the place where God had previously met with Moses. The thing that was missing from Elijah's life was worship. Take a good look at your life when you're stressed out and overwhelmed. It's very likely that your circumstances have caused you to quit spending time with God even if it's in the short-term. When Elijah couldn't see God working, he doubted. The trigger for this doubt and discouragement was exhaustion. He needed to trust God and believe that God was "saving a remnant" unto himself. He wasn't alone. The only way that he could truly trust God was if he stayed engaged with God. Having a regular, quiet time with God is absolutely necessary to remind you of a few things: *who God is, what he has done, and what he is continuing to do.* One of the important ways to rest is to spend time reading God's Word and praying. It's in this time of meditation that you slow yourself down to hear from God, kind of like that gentle whisper. If you're anything like me, you'd rather serve to see the spectacular. Remember, though, God is often found more in the quietness of simple obedience. This kind of a commitment will position you with laser focus for your life's purpose of glorifying God in all things. We need to be constantly reminded that a burnt-out Christian is no longer capable of seeing the truth until he prioritizes rest.

CHAPTER 10
FINDING QUALITY REST

Have you ever been so convinced of something, only to find out that you were completely wrong? I remember one time when I went to Menards with my wife. We were in the checkout line when I put my credit card into the machine for payment. It gave a strange beeping sound declaring my card to be ineffective. Frustrated, I stuck it into the machine again, receiving the same annoying sound. By this time, I was holding up the line, and I was really getting angry. I quickly pulled it out and stuck it in front of the cashier questioning why it wasn't working. She calmly and kindly declared to me that this is Menards, and the credit card that I was holding was a Home Depot card. Oh boy, was I embarrassed! My wife had a look of shame on her face, and I quietly pulled out my Visa card to make the transaction. As we left, I apologized and resolved to never let something like that happen again. Unfortunately, I am bound to do such a thing again. Why? Because I am human. In that moment, I was fully convinced I was right—until I wasn't! Have you ever had such an embarrassing experience?

One of the greatest mistakes that we tend to make is

that we often look in all of the wrong places for satisfying rest. As already mentioned, we fall into the trap of looking to people's expectations, to our own guilt, to boundary-less living, and to an absence of activity to give us true rest. Unfortunately, those things are like plugging a leak with your thumb. It's only a matter of time before anxiety, fear, and exhaustion comes rushing through those temporary fixes. God has given us the tools for a long-term fix. Throughout this book, my goal has been to remind you that rest is intrinsically connected to your purpose in Jesus Christ. If you try to short-cut rest, you will weaken your ability to live out that unique purpose. **Rest is a guaranteed component of endurance and influence.** It will help to bring you the confidence that you need to glorify God in your life.

Confidence is a powerful thing! As previously mentioned, the book of Hebrews is all about confidence in Jesus, proving him to be superior to all things including the angels, Moses, the first covenant (Old Testament sacrificial system), and even Israel's "rest" in the promised land of Canaan. Emphasis on the Levitical priesthood and on animal sacrifices support the conclusion that a community of believing and unbelieving Hebrews or Jews were the recipients of this letter. As intense persecution against the Hebrew Christians arose from traditional Jews, the Hebrews were tempted to cast aside any identification with Christ and in essence return to their old religious system. Here's what's happening: people called Judaizers believed that every Jew should continue to offer animal sacrifices and follow the Mosaic law. As a result, they peer-pressured many to follow their opinions rather than Biblical truth. The truth is that Jesus fulfilled the law and the prophets when he died on the cross and rose again from the grave.

Those animal sacrifices were but a foreshadowing of his work. He was the once-and-for-all sacrifice completing the first covenant of law with the second covenant of grace. The Judaizers were legalistic, meaning that they believed that their righteousness was measured by what they constantly were doing instead of what Jesus already did on the cross. They were in essence trying to replace "best" with their own version of religion.

We need to understand that there is no true rest without Jesus' completed work on the cross. Over the years, religion has offered many appealing opportunities that are ultimately bankrupt of "staying power." Have you ever heard of a hamster wheel? That's you trying to find rest apart from Jesus. Quality rest is found only in Jesus. We must prioritize it, or we will fall prey to religion's imitations. The plan for success takes us back to Hebrews 4 where we are reminded to handle these truths with care.

Have you ever dropped your cell phone only to see it shatter or crack? What about your fast food tray or grocery bags? We've all had these unwanted experiences. You think that what you're holding is stable in your hands, only to be reminded of how fragile life can be. I remember one time dropping my cell phone, and while it fell to the ground, I literally tried to use my shoe to break the fall. It didn't work, and because I don't have a case on my phone, you can guess what happened. The writer of Hebrews begins with a relatable admonition in Hebrews 4:1: "Therefore, since the promise of entering his rest still stands, let us be careful that none of you be found to have fallen short of it." Rest is achievable. **When you feel overwhelmed with no end in sight, remember that God offers a life-giving relationship with him.** It is your best option possible. Do you know the Savior? This question cannot be asked enough. The rest offered here for your soul impacts your mind and body. By trusting in Jesus' finished work on the cross, you can be saved from your sin unto the Savior! The Bible clearly states in Ephesians 2 that it's "by grace through faith" in Jesus and "not of anything you could ever do on your own." Maybe it's time that we take this question seriously. Jesus is the only way to true rest. Are you trusting in him not only for your day-to-day decisions but also for your eternal destiny? You are not taking rest seriously until you have done something to correct the lack of it. A spiritual lifestyle change is needed! It begins with a personal relationship with Jesus Christ.

The writer of Hebrews continues with a very important lesson. It's the cause-and-effect of what we do with knowledge. Think about this for a minute. Is there such a thing as "intelligent fear?" I would say "yes" to that question. I would also say that intelligent fear is a good thing. You might be thinking that so far I have come down very hard against fear, and you would be right, but there's a difference between unnecessary fear and necessary fear. For instance, if a big dog is chasing you, you are going to run because of fear. If a winter ice storm hits the road, you are going to drive slowly and cautiously because of fear. If you have a difficult exam or work presentation coming up, you are going to intensely prepare because of fear. In every case, fear was a motivating factor toward your desired success.

We are meant to learn from those who have gone on before us. Notice Hebrews 4:2: "For we also have had the good news proclaimed to us, just as they did; but the message they heard was of no value to them, because they did not share the faith of those who obeyed." The context of these verses is a reference to Numbers 13-14. Moses sends twelve spies into the promised land of Canaan to survey the land and their present opponents. Although this is a land that God had promised to Israel, they must have the courage to take it no matter what risks are in front of them. When the spies came back to Moses, they were overwhelmed with fear. Unfortunately for them, it was the wrong kind of fear. Instead of fearing missing out on God's blessings, they feared their opponents who were inferior to their God. They didn't see it. Instead, they saw "impossible" just like Elijah did. They failed to remember all that God had already done for them. They saw giants and fortified walls. They saw their own limitations. Out of the twelve spies, there were two men who trusted God. Joshua and Caleb pleaded with the people to "move forward" believing that God would overcome every obstacle that they faced, one at a time. Instead of listening, the people hesitated, complained, and gave up.

What God says he is going to do through us, we must not only believe, but we must also do! You can have all the information in the world, but if you're not putting action behind that information, you'll never spiritually succeed. I have known many people over the years that "knew" the Bible, but they never applied the deep truths of the Bible. Consequently, they were always constantly struggling in their journeys of faith. It doesn't have to be that way. That generation of Israelites allowed the "what ifs" to keep them from the amazing blessings of God. Will you make the same mistake? Remember, every decision that we make has a consequence attached to it. The offense that Israel was guilty of was faithlessness. They didn't trust God! God was not pleased. He held them accountable.

The next words of the writer should put a chill down our spines. Why? Because God hates faithlessness. Notice the consequences of Hebrews 4:3-5:

"Now we who have believed enter that rest, just as God has said, 'So I declared on oath in my anger, 'They shall never enter my rest.''" And yet his works have been finished since the creation of the world. For somewhere he has spoken about the seventh day in these words: 'On the seventh day God rested from all his works.' And again in the passage above he says, 'They shall never enter my rest.'"

It is not enough to know about; you must know with intention. The Israelites knew "about" God's good plan for them, but they couldn't bring themselves to believe that it could actually work. Stop fixating on the obstacles and start seeing Jesus the Overcomer! In today's church world, many churches are filled with people who know "about" God without *knowing God* based on a relationship that's grounded in radical faith. We claim to trust God until the challenge is greater than anticipated. We claim to follow God until the possible loss is greater than desired. We claim to love God until the sacrifice is too great.

We need to remember that God does all things well. When he demands sacrifice from your life, it's always in your best interest to comply. Why? Because God's plan for your life is better than anything you could ever think of for yourself. He is a God who brings complete and unadulterated joy and fulfillment. You can trust that he knows what he's doing with your life. Consider the illustration in the above text. After creating the world in six literal days, God rested on the seventh day to show that his work was completed, and he was fully satisfied with it (Genesis 1:31—"very good"). The earthly rest of Canaan was only a symbol of this rest. Therefore, the final rest in Hebrews 4 focuses on the perfect sacrifice of Jesus on the cross for you.

Remember the all-important words of Jesus in John 19:30: "When he had received the drink, Jesus said, 'It is finished.' With that, he bowed his head and gave up his spirit." What Jesus was saying is that he had perfectly completed God the Father's plan for the salvation of the world to those who would exercise saving faith. The spiritual rest that Jesus offers is perfect. There is nothing that could or should be added to it. God had completed his masterpiece.

Think about that from a creative perspective. Many people create through painting, drawing, woodworking, sewing, and so much more. That creativity comes from God. He is the author of the creative. God's "masterpiece of peace" was his finished work on the cross for you and me. Jesus brings satisfaction that will give you peace in every difficult circumstance now, with the hope of heaven later, as you begin to start handling your faith with more care. Are you trusting in Jesus for a quality of life that brings peace now and heaven later? As a result of their lack of faith, that generation of Israelites never received the promised land of Canaan. They never received their rest.

Unfortunately, there are some natural consequences of a faithless life to avoid. The first one is struggle. If you find yourself in a constant struggle, could it be because you have a hard time trusting God? We've already said so much in this book about trust, but it demands being repeated since it is the ultimate test of faith. Remember, fear controls our feelings as every decision, challenge, and unexpected event becomes a struggle. The second consequence of faithlessness is second-guessing. Perception controls our thinking, causing us to believe our decisions and experiences must be logical. Unfortunately, those mentalities are actually enemies of true Biblical faith. Don't be guilty of having to have all the answers before you put one foot in front of the other in action. There's no such reality. You and I will never have all of the answers before we make any decision. It's not possible. What is possible is God's blessing on our lives as soon as we act in faith, one step at a time. It terrifies me to think that the message of the Word of God could be of no value to me because I failed to act in faith. Missed opportunities lead to consequences. I want to avoid those consequences through a faith so deep that there is nothing that I won't attempt to do for the glory of God. My confidence comes in the fact that he has promised to empower me once I fully rely upon him. That is a recipe for mental and emotional rest.

One of the most common reasons that we miss opportunities from God is hesitation. Everything in life exists in a timeframe. Many years ago, I was having a conversation with a friend of mine about why he never married. He was in his mid-to-late 30s, and he was single. Now, don't get me wrong, there's absolutely nothing wrong with that, but what I learned is that he wished he was married. As the conversation deepened, I discovered that at one time he had been engaged, but it never worked out. I could feel his anguish explaining the story to me. I could sense his frustration with how things turned out. I can guarantee you that if given the same opportunity again, he would make sure that he married that girl. Unfortunately, life rarely gives those second chances. You have the opportunities within the timeframe in which they exist. If you hesitate, you might miss out. I can think of several times in my own life athletically, relationally, and even professionally when this truth played out. Thankfully, it was never in a life-altering situation. I never want to have to say, "If I had it to do over again, I would do it differently."

Don't hesitate; do it now! **Opportunities don't exist**

forever. Notice the words of the author as we continue to read in Hebrews 4:6: "[I]t still remains for some to enter that rest, and...those who formerly had the good news proclaimed to them did not go in because of their disobedience..." To the Christian, the door to "restful peace" is open to you today in spite of your circumstances. Rely on God and not on your own intellect, abilities, and personality. Create boundaries and accountability, removing all selfishness, fear, and hesitation. The opportunity exists right now. Will it always exist? Technically yes, but the deeper you get into disbelief, the harder it is to overcome it. You are not reading this book by accident. Some of you put on a "happy face" when you walk each week into your church building, although on the inside you are a chaotic mess filled with anxiety at the highest level. It's time to rest in Jesus! If you can trust him for your eternal destiny, you can trust him today. To the non-Christian, the door to restful peace is open to you today in spite of your current beliefs, priorities, lifestyle, and even confusion. Maybe you've grown up being taught that you have to "do things" to earn God's favor. Rest assured that you do not. Religion tells you to "do"; relationship tells you "done!" Jesus paid it all; all to him I owe! The religious leaders of Jesus' day and beyond taught that you had to follow the Old Testament sacrificial system and ceremonial laws even after Jesus had completed them. We call that legalism. Maybe, right now in this moment, God is exposing your emptiness through conviction that you must not ignore!

Twice a year, I see a dermatologist. My mother's side of the family blessed me with lots of moles. Therefore, I go and have them checked. Because it's a regular occurrence, I have developed a relationship with the doctor. He seems to genuinely care about me when I see him. He asks about my family, and we've had several conversations about my career. I am a pastor, and I love to invite people to my church. On more than one occasion, I have invited him. Unfortunately, he has never come. He tells me that he's not a religious man. I tell him neither am I. You should have seen his face the first time I said that to him. I proceeded to explain that it's not about man-made rules and regulations; it's about a living and powerful relationship with Jesus Christ. So far, it hasn't seemed to make an impact. Almost every time I invite him, he gives me some excuse. I remember the time that he told me that if he walked into a church it would "blow up!" I quickly corrected his thinking, declaring to him that everyone, including the pastor sitting in front of him, has issues. Still, he hasn't come. I have a burden for him. I've prayed about it. I've struggled with it. I long for him to give his life to Jesus. He has time…for now! But, when will that time be up? Each one of us has time until we don't have time. The key is living in urgency. If my doctor realized that he could die in a car accident on the way home from work and go to hell, maybe his response to my pleas would be different.

Urgency is the catalyst to change. The most important moment of your life is not next weekend or Christmas day or your next vacation; it's *right now!* We must make the most of each moment in life. Why? Because we're never going to get these moments back. What does God want you to receive right now from reading this book? For the Christian, it could be a change of lifestyle that ends up creating a trusting culture in your family. Don't you want your kids to trust God when difficult things come into their lives? Of course you do. Then start modeling what you want your kids to live out. One of the most powerful examples is the person who worships God in the struggle. He declares that

God is good not only in prosperity but also in problems. He faithfully serves the Lord when he is hurting emotionally, mentally, and even physically. He trusts God in the trials. We are called by God to live this way. Do it today! For the non-Christian, the urgent matter is to come to Jesus in saving faith. The Bible tells us that we are all sinners (Romans 3:10, 23). The Bible tells us that the payment for that sin is death (Romans 6:23). Thankfully, the Bible also tells us that there is a gift to receive (Romans 6:23; John 3:16; John 1:12; Romans 10:13). John 14:6 says, "Jesus answered, 'I am the way and the truth and the life. No one comes to the Father except through me.'" Will you call upon him to be your Savior, turning away from your sins? You can be gloriously saved right now! It will be the greatest decision of your life. If you make that decision today, I'd love to rejoice with you over it. Send me an email to john@weareemmanuel.life. I promise to personally pray for you the day I receive your email.

The author of Hebrews continues with this theme of urgency in the next verse. Notice Hebrews 4:7:

> "God again set a certain day, calling it '*Today*.' This he did when a long time later he spoke through David, as in the passage already quoted: 'Today, if you hear his voice, do not harden your hearts.'"

This quotation comes from Psalm 95:8-11. The context is of Israel overreacting to their circumstances. Instead of praying to God, they were complaining about God. Instead of anticipating God's provisions, they were overwhelmed with what they didn't have. They had been traveling in the desert, and they were thirsty but without water. Instead of trusting their leadership, they "contended" with Moses.

The word *contend* literally gives the idea of "bringing a lawsuit" against someone. In other words, they were seriously and emotionally distraught, and their distress led to irrational behavior. Sound familiar? Often, that is us when we allow anxiety and fear to control our thinking. In the end, God provided water for his people, but notice the indicting words of Exodus 17:7: "And he called the place Massah and Meribah because the Israelites quarreled and because they tested the Lord saying, 'Is the Lord among us or not?'" Massah literally means "test or prove," and Meribah means "strife or argue." They didn't trust God, and thirty-eight years later they'd come again to the place of having no water. Why would I mention that last thought? Be warned. God was not pleased when they had the attitude of "is the Lord among us or not?" The author of Hebrews cites this example as a warning against unbelief.

I try to think of it this way. There is a saying in our family that all three of my kids are familiar with. Over the years when I was on carpool duty, I would drop my kids off at school and always remind them, "There's no such thing as a throw-away day!" I would pray with them, and they would step out of my car into the "world." Why would I say such a thing? The reason is that I believed each day was going to have opportunities that they would never get back. I wanted them to have a sense of urgency to be kind, get good grades, achieve their goals, and, above all else, honor Jesus. I would challenge them to invite that "loner" to sit with them at lunch. I would tell them to pay close attention to their teachers. I would tell them to make a difference in someone's life in some way that day. I wanted them to live with urgency. Now, as I look back on those moments, I am so glad I challenged my kids in this way. They deeply understand how important each day is. They deeply understand how important it is to trust God with their present day, giving glory to His name.

The fact is that you can't do anything about tomorrow until you do something with today. Israel lived in a constant culture of faithlessness. It caused them only expanded grief and future loss. As I was scrolling up and down on my phone one day, I saw a Facebook post that said something like this: "If you don't prioritize taking your kids to church, they will seldom go when they are adults. Then, their kids will never go. Then, their kids' kids won't even know who God is!" Wow! That got my attention! Unfortunately, that is exactly what happened to the Israelites. Their parents' unbelief was passed down from generation to generation. **Faith is not a neutral, abstract concept. Faith is the defining characteristic of Christianity.** Everything that pleases or displeases God hinges on what we do with faith; therefore, we believe Jesus with everything that we are (Hebrews 11:6).

Sounds like a plan. It's what we strive to do as Christians. The reality is that we sometimes succeed. The most consistent reality is that we often fall short. What we need to remember is that we are on a journey of faith. When you fail to trust God, the last thing you ought to do is allow guilt to flood your soul. Instead, get back up. The next challenge is coming soon. That would be the next encouragement by the author in Hebrews 4:8-10:

> "For if Joshua had given them rest, God would not have spoken later about another day. There remains, then, a Sabbath-rest for the people of God; for anyone who enters God's rest also rests from their works, just as God did from his."

Remember Joshua? He was the spy who came back from Canaan trying to convince the people to trust God and take the land. He was later the leader of Israel when Moses died. After wandering in the wilderness for forty years because of their unbelief, Joshua led Israel into the land of Canaan. Finally, the perfect rest, right? Not so fast!

Will you ever get to the place in life where you have spiritually arrived? I want to emphatically say *no*. While we have the Holy Spirit living in us as Christians, we still battle with our sinful flesh. You will battle with sin until you're one day in heaven with Jesus. Prepare for the fight. Prepare for it every day. Even after Joshua (who is the "lesser" Jesus) led Israel into Canaan years later, the Israelites still had to fend off their enemies and deal with the daily grind of life. The author of Hebrews is reminding us that *nothing in this life* brings the ultimate rest that we always seem to be pursuing. The Sabbath-rest phrase was to take the readers back to the creation account and remind them that on the seventh day, God completed his perfect work and rested. While you will never find perfection until heaven, rest assured that you don't have to wait for heaven to find purpose. We do not have to wait for the next life to enjoy God's rest and peace; we can have it on a daily basis...right now! Our daily rest in the Lord will not end with death but will become an eternal rest in the place that Jesus is preparing for us right now (John 14:1-4). That is why living for Jesus in the present is a "touch of heaven" right now.

One of the things that we must make a priority in our lives is urgency. According to the Merriam-Webster dictionary, "Urgency is the quality or state of being urgent or insistent. It is also a force that compels or restrains." In other words, urgency makes the most of the moment. Urgency has a sense of timing. Urgency insists on living by a particular value system or motivational factor—right now. Urgency causes a person to be consumed with what he deems to be important. There are obvious examples, such as when someone you love is in a car accident. You want to know if he is going to be okay. You want to go and see him. You want to do it right away. There are also less obvious examples such as when you've procrastinated to get a certain project completed, like a school paper or a work contract, and now you have to rush to prepare in order to pass the class or seal the deal. Urgency tends to meet us when we are desperate. What if we flipped the script and made urgency a part of our lives from the start? What if we created some deliberate disciplines to help us achieve the kind of rest that restores our joy? That very subject will be our final chapter in this book. I intend to give you five absolutes that will help you "slow your life down" while accomplishing your full potential for Christ. Until then, let's take a look at the final thought of the author of Hebrews in this section.

Hebrews 4:11 says, "Let us, therefore, make every effort to enter that rest, so that no one will perish by following their example of disobedience." The author believed it was very important to approach life with urgency. His motivation was to avoid the discipline of God. His wisdom was to learn from the example of those who had previously failed. It begins with a serious examination of your faith in Jesus for salvation. Are you a genuine believer in Jesus? The importance of that question cannot be stressed enough. Do you have a growing awareness of God's presence and power, or are you fulfilling an "experience"? A state of urgency continues when we put forth the effort to experience spiritual rest now in the forms of peace, joy, and contentment. The effort that the author speaks of is not man-made strength; it is appreciating and benefiting from what God has already provided. That's the good news! Rest is at our fingertips if we will only take it. It is God's gift to us. A major part of this confidence available to us comes when we look forward to our heavenly future, which enables us to endure in the earthly present.

Sometimes before you can "find," you have to lose. You might be wondering what in the world does that mean. Well, remember the title of this chapter: "Finding Quality Rest." **Be willing to be discovered.** The Hebrews writer is "banking" on the power of God's exposing ourselves to us. Transparency seems to be a missing element in the American church. We are more concerned with our appearance than we are with our spiritual growth. We tend to desire acceptance at all costs. That's why so many Christians have bought the lie that they have no real issues. Fortunately, that's where the Word of God comes into play. Notice the polarizing words of Hebrews 4:12-13:

> "For the word of God is alive and active. Sharper than any double-edged sword, it penetrates even to dividing soul and spirit, joints and marrow; it judges the thoughts and attitudes of the heart. Nothing in all creation is hidden from God's sight. Everything is uncovered and laid bare before the eyes of him to whom we must give account."

God's Word has the ability to expose us. Sometimes, we really need that to happen.

God's Word, with amazing precision and purpose, cuts to the heart of our issues. It is more than simply a collection of words from various individuals. Instead, it is the lifegiving answer to our problems. It is living, dynamic, and active in our lives when we read and apply it. With the incisiveness of a surgeon's knife, it reveals who we really are and what we are not. It is able to penetrate to the core of our very being. It discerns what is within us even when others cannot see it. The tension that God's Word brings demands Godly decisions. It must shape our lives, and we must have a sense of urgency to allow it to shape our lives. By way of illustration, God's Word acts as a "spiritual mirror" reflecting to us the areas of sinful motivation and thought that no one else can see but you. You cannot hide anything from God. **Transparency is attractive.** Since God knows your "issues" and still loves you if you are his child, choose to trust him today and experience true rest.

Have you been searching for rest in all of the wrong places? Have you been ineffectively depending on yourself? Do you find yourself overwhelmed with no relief in sight? The chief culprit of your fatigue issues is faithlessness. If we trusted God, we would be able to sleep and would not be controlled by people's expectations of us; we would have true boundaries and would succeed with the wisdom that the author of Hebrews offers. **The key to rest is discipleship.** We must be growing in our relationship with Jesus, and in our final chapter we will highlight five practical ways to "make rest a reality." Are you ready? As they like to say on the athletic field after a big play, "Let's goooo!"

CHAPTER 11
THE ULTIMATE CHECKLIST

I don't know about you, but I am an ultimate checklist kind of person. My wife tells me that I'm OCD. Obsessive Compulsive Disorder is what it's called. I have never actually been diagnosed with OCD, but I have some tendencies in that way. One time a bunch of high school students found their way into my church office when I wasn't around. It was VBS week, and I was serving somewhere away from them. They proceeded to move books, glasses, folders, and even my precious sports memorabilia all around the room. They put my stuff in the oddest of places. I literally walked in on them doing it, and we had a laugh or two or a hundred after I threw them to the ground. I guess my youth ministry crazy side kicked in. One thing was for sure: it did actually bother me. Why, you might ask? It's because I am a person of extreme order. My wife thinks I'm crazy because I iron my jeans. My friends think I'm "over the top" because I am the opposite of most people. Instead of saving things, I actually really enjoy throwing things away. I'm telling you, my wife and I have probably kept the Salvation Army in business with all of the stuff that we have donated over the years. Probably the weirdest thing about me in my OCD tendencies is that I love to create lists. You might be thinking that isn't strange at all. Lots of people keep lists. Yes, but do those same people achieve tasks that weren't on their lists only to write them down after the fact, so that they can then cross them off a list they were never on to begin with? Yes, I know, it's a little weird—or a lot weird. You might not be as detailed or as organized as I am, and that's probably a good thing. Is it possible, though, that keeping a deliberate checklist will bring you the rest that you've been missing? The answer is a resounding "yes!"

As we conclude our journey through understanding and living out rest, there are five practical checklist items that need to be non-negotiable in our lives. In other words, if we apply these simple yet complex disciplines surrounded by the truth of God's Word, we will succeed at living a life of rest.

The first one is actually a marital counseling tip that I give to every couple who I have the privilege of meeting with, either before marriage or during their marriage struggles. You might be wondering what it has to do with rest, and the answer is everything. Check it out, and then I'll explain. **Organize the "organizable!"** One of the biggest thieves of rest is misinformation. That was exactly the issue with Elijah. He feared Queen Jezebel's threats because he was believing lies. There was a communication breakdown based on a lack of faith and focus. Having counseled hundreds of couples over the years, I see communication as a major culprit that leads to various dysfunctions. Often, trust is the greatest loss. Maybe one spouse can't trust the other spouse with money, while the other spouse can't trust her spouse with time or affection.

As a result, I counsel three aspects of organization to prioritize: finances, schedules, and expectations. Take the time at the beginning of every week to have a thirty-minute meeting with your spouse. Discuss the aforementioned areas. One of the largest causes of divorce is financial problems. Usually in a marriage there is a spender and a saver. The differences between the two can cause many issues. The key is healthy compromise. You're never going to have peace in your marital relationship if you don't plan to have peace. What I mean is that you must discuss the "nickels and dimes" before they create so much anxiety that you're overreacting in anger or fear. Then, there are your schedules. I can't tell you how many times I had plans for something that I didn't communicate to my wife. While she eventually found out about the plans, the breakdown in communication adversely affected the rest of the family's schedules. Maybe I missed one of my kid's games, or I wasn't available for something that she had planned. The point that I am trying to make is that it is tremendously important that we sync schedules with our families. As we've already discussed at length, everyone is going in a million different directions simply based on the "mad rush" of the American culture that we find ourselves engrossed in. Therefore, take the time to plan. Use that iPhone app called the "calendar" to schedule your life. You might think it's a small thing, but in reality it's a pretty big thing.

Last, there are your expectations for one another. What does my wife need from me this week? What does she expect from me this week? How can I be there for her this week? One of the biggest disappointments that I've seen in marriages over the years including my own is unmet expectations. We have this "happily ever after" mentality. The fact is that we've watched too many Disney movies. This is not how real life works. I don't sit on the couch gazing into my wife's eyes for hours listening to her every word. My wife surely doesn't sit in my man cave in the basement watching hours of hockey and football with me in her Michigan jersey wearing face paint. Don't you think she should? Okay, that was a joke, but you get my point. Every couple goes into marriage with a false set of expectations at some level. It takes some time for those expectations to "come down to reality." Unmet expectations can cause a great deal of stress, discouragement, and anxiety. That is why the sooner we talk to our spouse about our expectations the better. The reality is that we are both going to have to compromise in some areas. I've become a better listener over the years, and my wife has become more sensitive about my sports drive. While the above-mentioned scenarios are not realities, there are compromises that have been made to make our relationship stronger. Of course, there are hundreds of other more important examples of compromise that I didn't mention. The point is that you will never know what your spouse needs from you until you talk to her. In turn, she will never know what you need from her until she talks to you. Take the time at the beginning of your week to discuss these important areas. It's a thirty-minute commitment that is sure to relieve the stress of the other 167 hours and thirty minutes. Do it this week. You won't regret it.

The second checklist item is not going to be easy, but if you want to experience true rest, you'll prioritize it. **Say "no" more than you say "yes!"** We've already talked about boundaries. Let me remind you of how important they are, and then I'll give you some helpful hints on how to apply them. You can't be all things to all people. The sooner you realize this the better. Be warned that if you tend to care deeply about what others think of you, this is going to be a great challenge. Do you ever feel like your life is "under water"? If so, take inventory of your schedule and relationships. What you're going to find is that you are probably co-dependent on the love and acceptance of others. You feel as if when you say no, you're going to let that family member or friend down. Nothing could be further from the truth. The fact is that people tend to use the ones they love unintentionally. They might not mean to, but they are more focused on getting what they want than giving what you need. You need to convince yourself that saying no is not going to hurt your relationship with them. Honestly, if it does, the relationship is toxic anyway. Remember that exhaustion always leads to unhealthy vulnerability, and unhealthy vulnerability leads to anxious behaviors.

I told you that I'd give you a few helpful hints for how to apply boundaries in relationships. Here they are: 1.) Don't answer your phone "after hours!" 2.) Always know your family schedule! 3.) Never say "yes" without consulting! The fact is that there have been many times where my cell phone has rung after I've been home from work. I must be honest and admit there have been times when I have taken the call. In almost every instance, the conversation could have waited until the next day. Everyone has an "emergency!" That's code for, "I want you to fix my issues right now!" There's actually a lot to learn from patience and prayer. Obviously, there are instances of emergency like a death in the family, or a suicidal situation, or a devastating accident that must be instantly addressed. Everything else, however, can wait. A wise pastor taught me this truth years ago. Instead of answering your phone, let it go to voicemail, and then assess whether or not it can wait. Your family will appreciate knowing that they come first. In many cases, people are going to ask you to help them with something. They might even give you a date and a time of when they need the help. It becomes really helpful if you're able to instantly look at your calendar and see when your son's next soccer game or your daughter's next band concert is. That's why the first checklist item is so important. Have that thirty-minute meeting to start your week. Lastly, talk to your spouse before you say yes. There is absolutely no reason for you to have to give the asking person an answer on the spot. Often, we feel as if we need to, but when we do, we're saying that their need is more important than our family's feelings. Don't make this mistake! Don't make commitments on the spot! Instead, have a conversation with your family. Re-check the family schedule. Then, go back and tell your friend the answer.

Boundaries are extremely important. Your priority is to love God and love your family before all else. Your value is not found in what you do for others. Your worth is not found in the affirmation of others. Your responsibility is found in caring for your family first. Remember the warning of the Apostle Paul in 1 Timothy 5:8: "Anyone who does not provide for their relatives, and especially for their own household, has denied the faith and is worse than an unbeliever." The result of living with boundaries is the kind of rest that is free of people-pleasing. If you lose your family, it doesn't matter who else you've gained!

The third checklist item is the only way to live! If you choose to live in the alternative, you are likely to lose your mind on a regular basis. **Tackle the day, not your destiny!** We are all guilty of this day-dreaming disaster. We take our eyes off the moment and put it on the month. We take our focus off the short-term, which leads to long-term issues.

Remember the warning of Jesus from a very practical perspective in Matthew 6:34.

> "Give your entire attention to what God is doing right now, and don't get worked up about what may or may not happen tomorrow. God will help you deal with whatever hard things come up when the time comes" (*The Message*).

Compartmentalizing your life in this area is really important. It keeps you focused on the "immediate" first, which is the only appropriate way to deal with the future. There are a couple practical ways to do this. First, when your mind drifts, bring it back to the immediate. I tend to see Friday before I see Monday. The danger in that is that I'm taking all of my work and responsibilities for Monday, Tuesday, Wednesday, Thursday, and Friday and fearing that I won't be able to get all of it done. The issue with that is "depth perception." You might be thinking, *Huh? I don't get it.* I remember as a middle schooler playing a lot of volleyball. My youth pastor loved it, and he would take us on activities all the time where we were playing it. To make it more creative at times we played what was called "strobe volleyball." Literally, he would turn off the main lights and turn on strobe lights. Thankfully, we played with a beach ball instead of an official volleyball. The reason was depth perception. When you thought the ball was five feet from your face, it was actually five inches from your face. I can't tell you how many times I got smacked with a beachball to the old noggin. It was hilarious to see all of these "athletes" swinging at the ball and being way off. It wouldn't have been quite so funny if an actual volleyball would have been hitting us in the face. My point in the volleyball illustration is that what seems impossible is very possible. When I get overwhelmed with all that my week holds, I remember that all I need to be concerned about is today. Focus on today! If that seems overwhelming, reduce the day into segments or even hours. Win the day! Win the segment! Win the hour! Win the moment! Compartmentalize your life, and do it today.

The fourth checklist item is easy to ignore or even reject. You might even think that what I'm about to say is overrated. Many of you are not going to heed this warning, and you're going to eventually pay the price. **Go to sleep on time.** What I'm trying to say is that physical rest is a prerequisite for spiritual rest. God designed our bodies to need rest. We've already talked at length about the Sabbath Day that God made holy. He not only did so to show the completion of his perfect creation, but also as a model by which we are to physically rest from our work. In other words, you need breaks. You need vacations. You need time off. Almost all of us embrace what I just mentioned. Almost all of us struggle to get the daily rest that we need. My dad for years lived on five and a half hours of sleep per night. He would say that he wanted to spend the time with us kids and my mother. While I believe him, I saw the effects of that lifestyle on his body. If you want to be at your very best, you need to be rested. Your mind will be sharper. Your attitude will be better. Your productivity will be greater. Be disciplined in your sleep habits. You cannot "burn the candle at both ends!" There will be a consequence if you do!

When I was a youth pastor I took a mission trip to Mississippi to do hurricane relief. It was a difficult trip, as we worked in sweltering heat with high humidity. We stayed in trailers with minimal water and weak air conditioning. Because of how the trailers were set up, I had to split my group into different trailers. This mission trip involved other youth groups from other churches, so you can imagine how complicated it was to manage this whole thing. When I split up my group, one of the boys in my group decided that he was going to stay up all night for the next two to three nights. I'm talking 48-72 hours. Unfortunately, no adult in the other trailer did anything about it, and I was unaware of what was happening. In the next few weeks, this young man had a lot of mental and physical issues. He wasn't himself, and he had to be hospitalized for quite a while. The moral of the story is that while you might not think you need a lot of rest, God says otherwise. He created you to rest. While it is unacceptable to live a lazy, purposeless life, it is just as unacceptable to live a reckless, undisciplined life. It *will* catch up with you. Let's be honest, if you're not receiving healthy rest, you're probably already struggling in many areas. Don't make this unnecessary mistake. Turn off the TV! Get off your iPhone! Netflix can wait. Your company will be there tomorrow morning too. The ministry never ends. Get rest! Go to sleep! Do it right now! Ok, I'm kidding. Don't do it now, but do it at a reasonable time!

The fifth and final checklist item is a must. **Spend time with the one you claim to love.** Can you imagine claiming to love someone but wanting nothing to do with him or her? I love to spend time with my wife and kids. Right before I wrote this last chapter, I watched a Michigan basketball game with my son. The night before that I watched a *Cobra Kai* episode on Netflix with my girls. The point is that I love spending time with those I love. That last statement sounds obvious, doesn't it? A major part of that love must be built-in quality time. Who is a Christian commanded to love the most? The answer is God. Why then do we have such a hard time spending time with God? The fact is that you can apply a lot of practical tools that I have given to you throughout this chapter and even this book, but if you ignore this last point, you miss it all. God created us to be in a relationship with him. What that means is that you must proactively and deliberately make this a priority. At our church, our staff creates devotions to go along with the sermon series. Our *Celebrate Recovery* ministry picks a devotion to do each week that coincides with an aspect of their recovery emphasis. Our youth pastor offers different devotional books for our students. Our children's pastor links the *Orange 252* devotions to our website for our kids and their parents. Do you get the point? We highly value time spent in God's Word on a regular basis.

Let's face it, rest is hard to come by in our fast-paced, fast-food, fast-driving American culture. It is time that we slow ourselves down so that we can run an effective race. We have all seen runners who begin a race running with everything they have—arms swinging, muscles bulging, hearts racing. Instantly, they are out in front of the pack. It seems as though they can't lose, until they begin to wear down. Their lead begins to dissipate, and it's happening quickly. At this point in the race, the question is whether their lead was big enough from the start to get them to the finish line as champion. Instead of pacing themselves, they started with everything they had, only to eventually fizzle out. We've all seen runners who made that mistake. Personally, I tend to struggle with that temptation. I know many of you reading this book do so too, or else you probably wouldn't be reading it. Life is not a sprint; it's a marathon. My hope for you is that you will live with this warning in mind. How you start is important, but how you finish is even more important! My challenge for you comes down to this: Prioritize rest and watch God restore your purpose and joy. We are not meant to be overwhelmed with burdens; we are meant to be overwhelmed with God's goodness. It's time. You've waited long enough. There's a rest stop ahead.

ABOUT THE AUTHOR

With over twenty five years of ministry experience, John is a passionate leader who deeply cares about the spiritual journeys of people. Having been a youth pastor for 17 years, he understands the younger generation and is committed to impacting them. He is currently the pastor of a multi-site church in Genesee County, Michigan. He has been a featured speaker at several different ministry events including summer camps, young adult retreats, father & son retreats, and marriage retreats with his awesome wife of almost 25 years, Tamara.

To learn more about his life and ministry, visit johnscally.com.

www.ingramcontent.com/pod-product-compliance
Lightning Source LLC
Chambersburg PA
CBHW061748070526
44585CB00025B/2829